NORMAN SHAWCHUCK

VOLUME III

HOW TO MANAGE

CONFLICT
IN THE CHURCH

DYSFUNCTIONAL CONGREGATIONS

OW TO MANAGE CONFLICT
THE CHURCH:
ysfunctional Congregations

nted in the United States of America
st Printing 1996

blished By:

IRITUAL GROWTH RESOURCES®

ephone: (800) 359-7363

N 0-938180-16-9

MANAGING CONFLICT
IN
DYSFUNCTIONAL CONGREGATIONS

Table of Contents

INTRODUCTION

FAMILY SYSTEMS CONFLICT AND
HOW TO INTERVENE

I have worked as a management consultant in religious organizations for twenty five years, consulting hundreds of leaders and congregations in serious conflict. Out of this experience I prepared a *Conflict Management Learning System* for volunteer and professional religious leaders. The Learning System was initially comprised of two volumes. Volume I develops a theology of conflict in the church, gives resources for understanding how to respond to conflict as it escalates, and develops an understanding of how to manage conflict. Volume II presents a number of intervention models for intervening into church conflicts. The *Conflict Management Learning System* is valuable for anyone who wishes to become more effective in managing conflicts in the church.

In recent years I often confront a new type of conflict in the church which requires entirely new theories and interventions, if they are to be managed. This realization has dawned upon me slowly, as I found myself to be less than effective when dealing with certain conflict situations.

I began to take more care in analyzing the dynamics of these conflicts, and discovered that I was somtimes confronted by conflicts of an entirely different nature. This realization drove me to search the literature dealing with such topics as changes in American society, pastoral counseling, psycho-demographics, family systems theory (a relatively new field of science), addiction and leadership — when it is offered from the dark side of the leader's personality, the under-belly of the leader's experience.

What I learned I taught in my seminary classes, and wrote about in the books I authored. The feedback from my readers and students convinced me that I had to utilize new understandings and tools in those instances where earlier tried and proven approaches no longer were producing the results I wanted for my clients. This book is an update on my learning.

This is what I see: American society is becoming increasingly more broken. More broken homes, more crime, more drugs, more community alienation. These realities are new to us; breaking upon the American scene in the late 1960's, with the advent of national leaders who are openly dishonest, violent disruptions in communities, the displacement of employees through downsizing, the decline of the Mainline churches, to name a few disruptive changes in our society.

To state it simply, our society has become an addictive society. In the vortex of societal addiction denominations, congregations, leaders and people become addictive. The predominate reason people, organizations, institutions and society become addictive is that they are looking for a quick *fix* for their problems.

As I listened to the proceedings of the 1996 Democratic National Convention, I heard repeatedly that the welfare program, which President Clinton signed into law a week before the convention, is no good; it's flawed, it's broken. But, not to worry, "all we have to do is elect President Clinton to another term and he will *fix* it." All of this sounded a bit confusing to me. If the bill was no good why did the president sign it in the first place? And if it's so flawed, why do we think there's a quick fix to correct it? And if a quick fix was at the president's disposal, why didn't he take a few minutes to "fix it" before he signed the bill into law, or before the convention began?

Can it be that our entire political system has become addictive, and we, the codependent American people, are looking for quick fixes to problems that are not simple and will never be amenable to quick fixes? For example, in Robert Dole's 1996 campaign for the presidency he promised a 15% across the board tax cut. Is this also the promise of a "quick fix?" Is it also addictive?

All of society's addictions come into the church. The more a congregation succeeds in its mission to reach the lost, the alienated, the deeply disappointed persons on the fringes of our society, the greater and more intense will be its conflicts. Some of these conflicts are of an entirely new and different breed. In these situations the previous conflict management approaches we have utilized will not work; and in some situations will make matters worse.

How can we know whether we are facing a conflict that is more 'normal,' in which the more traditional approaches (as discussed in Volumes I and II of the *Conflict Management Learning System*) will suffice, or whether we are facing a conflict that is behaving more like an addictive system? For this question, there are no easy answers. However, I can give you a few clues. Here are some characteristics of conflict that arises out of addictive processes: denial, confusion, self-centeredness, dishonesty, lying, ethical deterioration, spiritual bankruptcy, hoping for a quick *fix*.

If you presently face such conditions, then this book is for you. But I caution you, for such conflicts there are no quick fixes. The good news is, however, if you find yourself in such conditions, then, left to themselves, matters will only get worse. This is a liberating thought. If you try something new and it doesn't work, neither will conditions improve if you don't try something new.

If you are striving to resolve a church conflict that leaves you confused, angry, getting your dossier in order, yearning for a more simple job — like working the fast pick-up lane at McDonald's, the chances are you are facing a type of conflict which this book addresses.

This book is for lay leaders as well as clergy. The day is past in which the pastor can resolve church fights on his or her own. The conflicts we face are too complex for one person to resolve. A new partnership of volunteer leaders and clergy is needed.

PREFACE

HOW TO MAKE THIS BOOK WORK FOR YOU

A process for getting the most out of your study of this book might be as follows:

- Begin by reading the book through in one setting.

- Study your way through the book, writing down new insights that come to you as you go. Also, jot down ideas that come to you, that you don't want to forget. The text pages provide you with blank space in which to write your jottings. If this is not enough space, use a notebook. Take all the time you need to read, think and write.

- Take some time between each chapter for mental digestion of the materials in the chapter. For example, take a day or two between the study of each chapter to let your ideas and learnings 'sink in' before proceeding with your study. However, you should not allow more than two or three days to pass before returning to your study.

- You will learn more if you study your way through this book with a group; perhaps your board members or key church leaders, or you might organize a group for this purpose. Be sure to provide each person his or her own copy of the book.

- Teach it! You will always learn more by teaching these materials to others. For example, you might offer a two to four session learning experience for interested persons in your congregation. This material not only works for congregations, it works for families too.

CHAPTER 1

INTRODUCING FAMILY SYSTEMS THEORY AND ORGANIZATIONAL DYSFUNCTION

The original inspiration behind the Franciscan movement came from words addressed to Francis from the cross at San Damiano in Assisi: "Francis, go rebuild my house which is falling into ruins."[1] Thomas of Celano

---

NOTICE!! You are about to embark on a study of a unique type of conflict in the church — conflict which arises out of dysfunctional relationships among the members of the congregation. What you will learn here will be so dramatic and powerful that you may be tempted to assume hereafter that all churches are dysfunctional, and all church conflict is also. This is not the case!

Some churches are dysfunctional. However, the majority of congregations have healthy relationships. These healthy churches are not considered in this book.

Most church conflicts are comprised of reasonably healthy and functional persons who get themselves into serious disagreements, many of which will not go away by themselves. In such instances, Interventions are needed to help persons work through their differences. Volumes I and II of the church *Conflict Management Learning System* deals with understanding and intervening into conflicts of this type; this is to say, conflicts involving persons who function more-or-less effectively in all of the important areas of their lives: home, work, social groups, and community. These persons may have serious disagreements and some outright fights. They are, however, socially and psychologically well adapted people.

This volume describes an entirely different type of church conflict which arises from dysfunctional relationships in the congregation. Dysfunctional relationships in the congregation are the result of emotionally or relationally damaged persons attempting to project their agendas upon the congregation. Often these are persons who are unable to function well in many areas of their lives: family, job or community. Some such persons occasionally 'retreat' to the church; from which they will make "their last stand," attempting to find some area in their lives in which they can command the right to influence

notes

and dominate. This is not always the case, however, for persons may function more-or-less adequately in the other areas of their lives, and yet be dysfunctional in the congregation.

There is another avenue by which dysfunction comes into the church. This is by reason of outreach ministries proving to be successful in reaching the broken and marginal persons in society. These persons may come to the church, be given new life, and yet bring all of their dysfunction with them. This phenomenon is somewhat analogous to the raising of Lazarus from the dead, who was given new life and yet came dragging all of his grave clothes with him. Lazarus was alive, but yet bound. Jesus said it was the responsibility of those who believed to set him free.

Dysfunctional conflict, as referred to in the preceding paragraph, requires a new theory and unique interventions, in order to understand and manage it. The new theory is termed *Family Systems Theory*. The interventions grow out of its understandings. This book will discuss the theory and point the way to intervening into dysfunctional conflict in the church.

Family Systems Theory, as applied to congregations, is based upon the premise that congregations are made up of families, and, in many important ways, the congregation behaves like a family. Members of a congregation may have deep emotional investments in their relationships with one another. In addition, the church is one of the few institutions that hosts the entire family in its life and ministry, as well as the individual's entire life cycle — from birth to death. Family Systems Theory is a recent development that greatly assists therapists and pastoral counselors to understand and treat dysfunctional families.[2]

DYSFUNCTIONAL CONGREGATIONS

When the congregation is a healthy system, individual members thrive because of the empowering influence of the life of the body. When the congregation is unhealthy, our efforts to equip a few motivated individuals are usually doomed.[3]

There are four guiding principles which help us understand the possible extent of dysfunction in the congregation, or in a member's life:

1. *Persons who are competent in all other areas of their lives might be dysfunctional in the church,* because the church is a unique system that takes on many characteristics of a family.

2. *Often a relatively small group is dysfunctional in a church, with the rest of the people being competent.* It is not often that everyone in the congregation is dysfunctional.

3. *An entire congregation can become dysfunctional.* This is more often the case in smaller congregations, but it also happens in large churches. Obviously, not all of these people are dysfunctional in all other areas of their lives, but as members of the church family system they all engage in dysfunctional behavior.

4. *Dysfunction in a congregation is often passed on from generation to generation.* The current dysfunctional behaviors in the congregation are likely to be the results or reflections of dysfunction in previous generations.

The congregation-as-a-whole may become dysfunctional through the process of taking in new people who are dysfunctional in one or more areas of their lives, and who introduce this dysfunction into the congregation. For example:

1. The congregation hires a pastor who is dysfunctional

2. Persons who are dysfunctional become new members

3. An influential member may experience a series of 'breakdowns' in his or her life (family, job, health) and project the results of these breakdowns onto the congregation.

However, not all dysfunction need be introduced from the outside. The congregation-as-a-system may become the carrier of dysfunction. For example:

1. The congregation may feel unable to cope with a succession of rapid and/or radical changes in its community; thus becoming highly anxious and paralyzed to act.

2. Recurring cycles of threatening conflict may break out in the congregation which it is totally unable to resolve. Over time, the stress and anxiety move the congregation to dysfunction.

An underlying characteristic of virtually all dysfunctional persons is that in earlier generations of his or her family there has been a history of dysfunction: addictions, co-dependence, divorce, a pattern of losing, etc. Dysfunction is usually (but not always) a family affair spanning generations.

This is also true for the congregation. Often dysfunction in a congregation has been passed on from one generation to the next, perhaps becoming dormant for several years, only to reappear at a later time. Consider the following example:

> A father of two young daughters, the board chairperson of the congregation which he and his family attended, sought counsel when he learned that a year previous a senior member of the congregation had sexually molested the pastor's young daughter. The pastor, however, had decided "for the sake of the ministry" not to disclose the incident and had instructed his daughter to tell no one.
>
> After one year the pastor's daughter told the board chairperson's daughter — who then told her father. The board chairperson talked to the pastor. The pastor begged him to tell no one, stating that if the incident became public, it would ruin the church.
>
> The board member was distraught and went to the only psychologist in the area for help. The psychologist, a long time therapist in the community, told him that over the past thirty years she had heard of many such incidents in the congregation. She had spoken to several pastors over the years who, upon learning of the incidents, had chosen to leave the congregation without making the situation public.
>
> Now the board member was filled with fear that the same thing might happen to his own daughter, but he did not want to make the incident public since the pastor begged him not to do so, and he worried that if the story got out it would ruin the church.

This story illustrates that dysfunction in a congregation can span generations and yet never become known. A dysfunctional congregation will do almost anything to keep from disclosing "the family secret." Further, a dysfunctional congregation seems to possess an uncanny ability to hire pastors who are also dysfunctional in some areas of their lives, and who are, therefore, very good at keeping "family secrets."

The dysfunctional behavior in this church was able to continue because there was always someone in the congregation who was willing to play the co-dependent role,[4] which is necessary if the dysfunction is to remain hidden, and the addictive persons are to be protected from the full responsibility of their behaviors. The co-dependents in this case included the pastors who left without disclosing the dysfunction and, undoubtedly, other members who knew, but kept the 'secret.' The story describes a severely dysfunctional congregation in which various members filled crucial roles that allowed the dysfunction to continue over generations. Not all dysfunctional congregations are so dysfunctional. Dysfunction comes in degrees. Many exhibit no dysfunction at all. Others are highly dysfunctional. Many others fall somewhere in between. Figure 1.1 is a matrix depicting the possible range of relational health in a congregation, from Highly Competent to Severely Dysfunctional relationships:[5]

Figure 1.1

Quality of Interpersonal Relationships Within the Congregation

Capable negotiation, Warmth, Intimacy, Humor	Ambivalence not recognized, Warm relations then control struggles, Negotiation with pain, Neurotic	Conflict is hidden not obvious, Committed to relationships but no closeness, Warmth in relationships ranges from High to Low	Chaotic, Tyrannical control, Rigid, Depressed, Outbursts of rage, Obsessive	Confused Communications, Lack of shared Focus, Despair, Cynicism, Schizophrenic
Highly competent				Severely dysfunctional
	Competent but pained		Conflicted	
		Complementary dominant-submissive		

PRINCIPLES OF FAMILY SYSTEMS THEORY APPLIED TO THE CONGREGATION

When a congregation is under stress or not meeting the needs of its members, the anxiety does not occur solely because of one person. This condition has more to do with how people relate to each other. Stress and anxiety are a family affair. Therefore, in order to understand the behaviors of individual members, it is important to see how persons function in their own family contexts. What is the person's family like? How do the family members communicate? What are the family rules? What are their beliefs and values? How are individuals' needs met? Who is the keeper of the family traditions? The answers to these questions give clues to understanding the behaviors and attitudes persons bring with them into the church.

notes●
notes

These same questions can also be asked of the individual's other relational systems: the work place, the community, close friends. Understanding the individual's 'place' and relationships with his or her family or companions give important clues as to how the person will relate to the congregation.

The five basic principles of systems theory

There are five basic principles that form the foundation for family systems theory, as it might be applied to congregations. All that follows in this book are built upon these principles. These systems principles form the foundation for working with a congregation in conflict. It is essential, therefore, that you keep them in mind as you study your way through this book, and especially when you study Chapter 5, "Intervening in Dysfunctional Congregations." Hereafter, when you plan interventions for your church, base them upon these principles. The principles are:

• *The congregation as a whole is greater than the sum of its parts.* When members are together, they respond according to the emotional dynamics going on in the group at that time. When taken out of the group context, an individual may behave differently.

• *If you change one part of the congregation system, you change the entire congregation.* A change in one part of the congregation system will affect all other parts. The congregation has to adjust to the change one member may bring; for example, when that person refuses to play old games, or relates to other members outside of the norms held by the congregation.

• *Systems become more complex and organized over time.* Each day brings new problems, information and opportunities to the congregation. As such, the congregation is dynamic and changing as it grows more complex over time. The congregation must grow, adapt and adjust to the changes in its environment, as well as its internal changes, if it is to survive.

• *The congregation is open, changing, goal directive and adaptive.* The congregation has resources within its own ranks to deal with internal needs as well as external threats and opportunities. It also has potential for coming up with its own strategy to meet its challenges.

• *Individual dysfunction is a reflection of an active emotional system.* Conflict and anxiety in the congregation do not occur solely because of the personal struggles of one person or group. Problems have more to do with relational networks and how individuals function within those networks. When a certain member's behavior is dysfunctional, it serves a role model for other members who will reciprocate with dysfunctional behaviors of their own. These reciprocal roles are established over time and become normative and predictable among the members. These dynamics may contribute toward an inability of a group or the congregation-as-a-whole to move toward relational or spiritual healing and effectiveness. Individuals or groups become stuck in their dysfunctional patterns. [6]

TIME OUT

FOR A MENTAL DIGESTION

1. How would you describe family systems theory in your own words?
2. How would you describe dysfunction in your own words?
3. What are some of the ways that a congregation becomes dysfunctional?
4. Study the continuum of interpersonal relationships, on page 7:
   • Which of the stages best describes your congregation?
   • What could you do to move the congregation into a more healthy stage?
5. Review the five basic assumptions of Family Systems Theory. Where do you observe these assumptions in your family? In the congregation? List at least one example for each assumption.
6. Do you see evidence of dysfunction being passed on from one generation to another in your congregation? How about in your family? In your spouse's family?
7. In reflecting upon this chapter, what stands out in your mind as the most important thing to remember as you work with your congregation?

[1] Michael H. Crosby, *The Dysfunctional Church: Addiction and Co-dependency in the Family of Catholicism* (Notre Dame, IN: Ave Maria Press, 1991), p.97.
[2] The theorist who has most comprehensively applied family systems theory in religious organizations is Edwin Friedman. See his landmark text, *Generation to Generation: Family Process in Church and Synagogue* (New York: Guilford Press, 1985).
[3] R. Paul Stevens and Phil Collins, *The Equipping Pastor: A Systems Approach to Congregational Leadership* (Washington, DC: The Alban Institute, 1993).
[4] The co-dependent person or group gains his or her fulfillment in life from caring for, making excuses for, an addicted person or group. The co-dependent is addicted to taking care of addicts.
[5] Adapted from Jerry Lewis, *The Birth of the Family*, (New York: Brunner/Mazel, 1989.) pp. 164-166.
[6] Adapted from the work of David S. Freeman, *Techniques of Family Therapy* (New York: Jason Aronson, 1981), pp. 18-27.

GREAT

resources

CHAPTER 2

THE BUILDING BLOCKS OF A DYSFUNCTIONAL CONGREGATION

Congregations (or families) do not become dysfunctional for no reason; nor do they become dysfunctional over night. A congregation moves from greater degrees of health to increasing degrees of dysfunction only in the presence of certain conditions, which must come together to form the relational climate in which dysfunction is allowed to grow. These conditions are: addictive behavior, codependent behavior, the identified patient (symptom bearer) and participation in series relationships. These are the building blocks of dysfunction:

ADDICTIVE BEHAVIOR

[An addiction is] *any **substance** or **process** that has taken over our lives and over which we are powerless. It may not be a physiological addiction. An addiction is any process or substance that begins to have control over us in such a way that we feel we must be dishonest with ourselves or others about it. Addictions lead us into increasing compulsiveness in our behavior.*[1]

Anything can become addictive. Anything you would feel you had to lie about under direct questioning is likely an addiction.

Addictions can be formed from the abuse of *chemicals* (i.e., drugs, alcohol, nicotine, caffeine). They can also be formed from the abuse of *processes* (i.e., religion, sex, money, work, conflict, power).

What is surprising at first glance is that *process addictions serve the same function as a chemical or substance addiction*. The addiction serves to alter the mood of the individual or group so that they might escape unwanted feelings and/or anxiety by numbing the person so that he or she is out of touch with what he or she knows or feels in those momentary times of greater 'sobriety' or realism.

COMPULSIVE BEHAVIOR

Compulsion is a special form of process addiction. It is characterized by workaholism, perfectionism, the insistence that others submit to his or her way of doing things, dogmatism, obstinacy.[2]

notes

A common expression of compulsive behavior in the congregation is the senior pastor demanding that all other pastors and staff pledge their blind loyalty to him, even when his directions or policies are wrong, dangerous or questionable.

Gerald May describes the dynamics that move one to addiction, or compulsive behavior:

> *The longing at the center of our hearts repeatedly disappears from our awareness, and its energy is usurped by forces that are not at all loving. Our desires are captured, and we give ourselves over to things that, in our deepest honesty, we really do not want. ... Theologically, sin is what turns us away from love; away from love for ourselves, away from love for one another, and away from love for God. When I look at this problem, psychologically, I see two forces that are responsible: repression and addiction. We all suffer from both repression and addiction. Of the two, repression is by far the milder one. ... While repression stifles desire, addiction attaches desire, bonds and enslaves the energy of desire to certain specific behaviors, things, or people. These objects of attachment then become preoccupations and obsessions; they come to rule our lives.*[3]

CODEPENDENT BEHAVIOR

Addictive relationships must have at least two parties to play out the dysfunction: the *addict(s)* and the *codependent(s)*. While the addict uses a substance or process to escape from his or her unwanted feelings, the codependent stabilizes the situation so it doesn't collapse, and prevents the addict from feeling the full consequence of his or her behaviors. Both the addict and the codependent surrender their own integrity and inner life in order to keep the relationship in tact.

Every addict needs a codependent to protect him or her from the full weight of the ultimate outcome of continuing the addiction. On the other hand, every codependent needs an addict in his or her life, in order to feel worthwhile.[4] The codependent measures his or her sense of self-worth by the extent to which he or she is able to provide a circle of safety in which the addict may continue the addiction.

The codependent may be described as follows:

Codependents will "cut out their center" — that core of self that can think, feel, decide, and act — and hand that center over to someone else, either to another person, or to the family, or to some institution or system. The codependent then acts by "remote control," taking cues not from the inside, but from that other source. ... They will cling to this substitute-center even when the thoughts, feelings, and actions it dictates begin to destroy their lives. They will hold on as if survival depended on it, as if they had no other choice.[5]

The goal of the addict is to continue the addiction, while the goal of the codependent is to keep everything in order so that the addiction may continue. As destructive as addiction and codependency appear from the outside, they fulfill an important need for the persons involved — they insulate people from true reality, and deaden their feelings.

In the final analysis there is no difference between the results of addiction or codependency. Both the addict and the codependent are addicted. The addict is addicted to the addictive process or substance, while the codependent is addicted to the process of protecting the addict. Since both addiction and codependency are part of the addictive process, the codependent expression supports the addictive dimension at all levels and, in turn, codependents are rewarded by the addictive system for their loyal support. Both are dysfunctional.

Dysfunctional persons, whether in the home or the congregation, re-enact their own pain on those around them in several different ways, including control, aggression, crisis orientation, self-centeredness, unresolved issues that go on for years, judgmentalism, rigidity, gossip, unreliability and perfectionism.

IDENTIFIED PATIENT (SYMPTOM BEARER)

When anxiety increases within a congregation, persons unconsciously attempt to "purify" themselves by locating the problem in another individual or group. Once the clergy, or board, or the majority of the congregation is able to tag some person or group as the cause of the problem, they can absolve themselves of any responsibility for the results of the problematic behavior. Now they are able to say, "They" have a problem. Or, better yet, "They *are* the problem." This person or group now becomes the "identified patient" or "symptom bearer" of the congregation.

At closer look, however, the individual or group issues are almost always the results of dysfunction within the congregation itself.

> *Dysfunction is a family affair. An individual or group in a congregation is not able to perpetuate dysfunctional behavior unless the leaders or the congregation-as-a-whole already possess dysfunctional characteristics.*

Picking someone to be the 'symptom bearer' in the congregation (so that the rest of the people need not feel any sense of responsibility or blame) is a time honored tradition in religious organizations. In the Old Testament, for example, the priest would select a scapegoat upon which the congregation would heap its annual collection of sin and transgressions. The priest would then lead the Symptom Bearer into the desert and kill it as an atonement for the congregation's sins and failures. In medieval times, a community in stress would identify someone as the "witch" and burn him or her at the stake in order to purify the community. Today, the leaders of the congregation, and many of its members, transfer their own problems or deficiencies onto someone else. "If only this person or group would leave the church, then our problems would be over."

Many dysfunctional congregations, or a dysfunctional group within the congregation, will attempt to identify the pastor, or the pastor's spouse, as the identified patient. In fact, dysfunctional congregations seem to have an uncanny ability to hire a new pastor whom they hope to make the identified patient. In such instances the pastor already possesses sufficient dysfunction to make him or her a likely candidate for the role. This is what we will observe in the case presented later in this chapter.

The attempt to make the pastor, or the pastor's spouse, the identified patient is much like the practice of the ancient Hebrews, who used a scape goat to bear their symptoms. Even as the Hebrews piled their sins and shortcomings upon the goat and then killed him, some congregations hope to make the pastor their scape goat, and then fire him or her. The end result is the same in both instances.

notes

24

However, the symptom bearer is not necessarily the "sick" member of the congregation. *The congregation-as-a-whole is the carrier of the illness.* Merely identifying one person or group as the carrier of the illness may provide a temporary relief, but it does not affect a lasting remedy.

The symptom bearer is the one in whom the congregation's anxiety has surfaced and has been expressed. Such symptoms, therefore, are the expression of relationships, organizational structures, and processes within the congregation. Congregations can easily get caught up in blaming someone else for their troubles, with no one being willing to take responsibility for his or her part. A beginning sign of health is when persons and groups stop blaming others and begin to take responsibility for their own involvement in the congregation's conflict and/or illness.

Keeping the focus on a "problem" person or group prevents the congregation from addressing the systemic issues that contributed to the symptoms in the first place. Under such conditions, essential change toward health is not likely. The symptoms will recycle in the same or different persons and as the same or different issues. This is because the systemic context of the "problem" person or group has not been addressed.

This points to an important principle for intervening in a dysfunctional congregation: *It may not be best to deal with the symptom bearer.* Rather, the most effective intervention will likely be with the most healthy *person or group who has the capability to bring positive change* to the congregation. It is also worthwhile to help persons deal with issues in their own family, or with their own jobs, which they may be projecting onto the concerns of the congregation. This intervention principle will be discussed at greater length in Chapter 5 of this book.

In sum, the symptom bearer is not *the* problem. The symptom bearer becomes the most obvious expression of problems more deeply enmeshed within the congregation; its relationships among members, the way it is organized for work and ministry, and the way it goes about its work and ministry.

When a congregation comes under serious stress, it often will try to transfer its anxiety upon a person or group which becomes the *identified patient* for the congregation. Then the rest of the members have a scape goat for themselves; "I may be causing *some* of this trouble, but he is really the one who is destroying the church! If only he would leave, then all our problems would be over." This is never the case!

SERIES RELATIONSHIPS

A series relationship occurs when persons cannot act independently of one another. People in a series relationship are not *together* so much as they are *stuck together.* Whatever one person in this *stuck together* group thinks or does, all the other people in the group will do the same, since they have no capacity to think critically about the behavior of the person who is setting the agenda.[6]

Persons who become a part of a series relationship are dysfunctional, and such persons in the congregation find one another. They *need* each other, because they get their energy from the relationships they have with the group. The dysfunctional group will go to all lengths to make certain that no one leaves the group, because they fear that if one person leaves the group, all the others will lose their energy source. This is why they feel they must stay together; they must remain *stuck together.*

As a stuck together group they can act in ways that paralyze the rest of the congregation. They often succeed in becoming a powerful, influential block that sets the agenda for the congregation for years on end. This happens because their behavior is so offensive that the other members of the congregation feel it might be unchristian to intervene into the lives and behaviors of these members. And so the congregation panders these people; "after all, they are members of our congregation, and we don't want to hurt them." However, the persons in the series relationship know no shame. They will take all the pandering they can get — so long as they are allowed to set the agenda for the church.

In this condition the dysfunctional group acts as the addictive party while the rest of the congregation plays the codependent role. And they are not aware that they are playing the role of the codependent. Often the people in the congregation are totally oblivious to the fact that it is their codependent behavior that makes it possible for the stuck together group to continue. Consider the following case:

CASE STUDY

A congregation of 650 members found themselves in need of securing a new pastor. A search committee was appointed to do the leg work. The committee was headed by a man who selected the rest of committee members. He appointed five women to serve on the committee.

The denomination provided the committee some fifty dossiers of pastors who were available to serve congregations. The committee chairperson went through the dossiers and announced to the rest of the committee that he had found a candidate who was so good that they should hire him immediately. The committee members questioned whether it was wise to hire a pastor sight unseen, and it was not in keeping with the congregation's policy. The chairperson responded by saying that the candidate was so good he would certainly be hired by some congregation very soon, and that he would convince the church board that immediacy required a breach of church policy.

The committee agreed. The chairperson convinced the church board to go along with the committee's wishes. The pastor was hired.

Six weeks after the new pastor had arrived, the committee chairperson informed the board that the congregation had made a terrible mistake in hiring the pastor, and he must be terminated immediately. The board asked why. The chairperson responded that the reasons were so sensitive he could not share the details with them. The board refused to hear any more of the matter.

The following Sunday the committee chairperson announced to the congregation that the pastor was very bad, and the congregation should remove him immediately.

The pastor refused to leave. The leader of the women's group launched a crusade to get the pastor out. A group of older women in the women's organization immediately joined with her. This group of women marched into the pastor's office and demanded that he be out of the parsonage and out of town by the next day. The pastor threw them out of the office. The women escalated the conflict until the women, the board, the church staff and others were locked in mortal combat.

After about six months the pastor resigned and left, but not before preaching his last sermon on demonic possession. He told the congregation there were demon possessed people in top leadership positions and that a cloud of judgment and hell hung over all their heads. Then he walked off the platform and out of the building, got into his car and left. The congregation never saw or heard from him again.

The denomination called upon a consulting agency to help figure out what had happened in the congregation. The consultants conducted one hundred private interviews with members of the congregation. Throughout the course of the interviews a number of women reported that they had been sexually molested by the chairperson of the search committee. These incidents spanned nearly two decades.

All of the women whom this man had selected to be on the search committee were among those reporting they had been sexually molested by him. None of the married women of the group had told their husbands.

The consultants did a background check on the pastor who had left. He had been accused of sexual molestation in his previous church. The woman and her husband did not want the matter to go public. The pastor agreed to leave, the board agreed to tell no one, and the couple pressed no charges.

In the chapter we have discussed the building blocks that move a congregation toward greater degrees of dysfunction. In Chapter 3, following, we will discuss the results of these building blocks within the life of a congregation.

TIME OUT

FOR A MENTAL DIGESTION

1. Study the case on pages 26-27 to identify which of the building blocks of dysfunction are present. Also identify each person or group who was building the blocks into the relationships within the congregation.
2. Which, if any, of these dysfunctional behaviors do you see in your congregation, in the families of key leaders, influential members? Describe the behaviors. What is the result of these behaviors within the congregation?
3. If you discover signs of dysfunction in your congregation, thoroughly review your own behavior in the dysfunction:
   • Are you addicted to a process? To a substance?
   • Are you filling a codependent role for an addicted person? If so, why are you filling this role? Think the answer through very carefully.
   • Is the congregation, or a group, attempting to use you as an Identified Patient (a Symptom Bearer)?
   • Are you participating in one or more series relationships? If so, what steps will you take to break the series relationship?
4. (This will take some time and work. You need not do it now. But when you do it, it will be worth the effort.) Construct a family history of your extended family, and your spouse's family. Identify the persons in each generation that exhibited dysfunctional behavior. How were these behaviors, or the results of them, passed on to succeeding generations? How are they effecting your nuclear family? (Remember: not every family has dysfunction. Do not pretend what isn't there. Be honest.)[7]

---

[1] Anne Wilson Schaef and Diane Fassel, *The Addictive Organization*, (New York: Harper & Row, 1988), p. 58ff.
[2] Anne Wilson Schaef and Diane Fassel, *The Addictive Organization*, p.82.
[3] Gerald G. May, Addiction & Grace (San Francisco: Harper & Row, 1988), pp. 1-3.
[4] For this reason 75% of spouses in the United States who divorce an alcoholic, when they marry again will marry another alcoholic.
[5] Virginia Curran Hoffman, *The Codependent Church* (New York: Crossroad, 1991), p.23.
[6] See Edwin H. Friedman, *Generation to Generation: Family Process in Church and Synagogue*, pp. 25-26.
[7] For aids to construct your family history, see Edwin H. Friedman, *Generation to Generation*, "The Idea of a Family," pp. 11-39, and Monica McGoldrick, *Genograms in Family Assessment*, (New York: W. W. Norton & Company, 1985).

GREAT

resources

CHAPTER 3

THE RESULTS OF DYSFUNCTION IN THE CONGREGATION: THE BREAKDOWN OF HEALTHY RELATIONSHIPS

Chapter 1 introduced you to Family Systems Theory, and to a unique type of conflict termed Dysfunctional Conflict. In Chapter 2 you were introduced to the "building blocks" (the dysfunctional dynamics) that move a congregation into dysfunction.

The results of the 'building blocks of dysfunction,' discussed in the previous chapter, are experienced most graphically in the interpersonal and intergroup relationships within the congregation. These results serve to distinguish dysfunctional conflict from other conflicts which arise out of organizational disagreements. Conflicts which arise between more healthy persons and groups always begin by focusing upon organizational structures, goals or programmatic concerns. The focus will remain upon such concerns if the conflict is well managed. If the conflict is not well managed, as the tensions increase the group will move into injustice collecting and confrontation. These dynamics are discussed in Volumes I and II of the church Conflict Management Learning System.

Your attention is now directed to the *results* of the "building blocks" (the dysfunctional dynamics) upon the intrapersonal and interpersonal relationships within a congregation.

As a congregation moves from being a healthy organization into more dysfunctional behavior, the quality of its relationships (interpersonal and intrapersonal) erode more and more. The focus of dysfunctional conflict is always upon relationships. The issues in dysfunctional conflict always has to do with relationships. The issues may *appear* to focus upon organizational concerns, but underlying the reality of dysfunction in relationships, whether intrapersonal or interpersonal. Figure 3.1, next page, illustrates the patterns of relationships in a healthy and an unhealthy congregation:[1]

Figure 3.1

Patterns of Relational Health in Dysfunctional and Healthy Congregations

Intrapersonal/Group Dysfunction		Relational Health: Functional Behavior
	ANXIETY	
Denied, habitual, chronic		Brought to light and addressed
	BOUNDARIES	
Closed, rigid, enmeshed, co-dependent		Fluid, balance between self and others
	EMOTIONS	
Suppressed, out of control, detached		Expressed in responsible ways
	TRIANGLING	
Suppressed feelings, detached, people triangle others		People own up to own feelings, appropriate self disclosure
	HOMEOSTASIS	
Vicious, recurring cycles, resistance		Proper balance, interdependence

A healthy congregation can get into serious conflict, experience anxiety, get caught up in some emotional triangles, have boundary issues and experience high emotions. However, in a healthy congregation, these concerns can be managed and actually work for the greater health of the congregation.

In a dysfunctional congregation, however, these same concerns spin out of control, so that an individual or group may become exceedingly anxious – even overwhelmed by anxiety. Emotional triangles may be found popping up everywhere — virtually all of them aimed toward dragging the pastor (and other key leaders) into them. Boundaries range from totally rigid to being totally enmeshed. Emotions run at a fever-high pitch, and homeostasis is maintained by vicious cycles recurring around the same issues which are never resolved. The results of dysfunctional conflict will now be addressed:

FEVER-HIGH ANXIETY

So do not worry about tomorrow, for tomorrow will bring worries of its own. Today's trouble is enough for today. (Mt. 6:34)

In every significant relationship, people will experience tensions and anxiety. In a healthy congregation, anxiety acts as an alarm system, signaling people that something is not right, that there is a potential crisis. When anxiety has a rational basis and is controlled, the anxious moment presents the opportunity for relationships to change and grow. Therefore, anxiety can at times be the lifeline of relationships in the congregation.

In a dysfunctional congregation, however, anxieties run continually at a fever high pitch for some person or group. Always someone is gripped with anxiety, fearing the absolute worst thing possible is going to fall upon the congregation. Such anxiety paralyzes people to change or to respond to the anxious moment.

Anxiety in a troubled congregation is most often released in a free floating manner and finally 'lodges' in persons who are most vulnerable. This anxiety has no focus. Its free-floating, erratic influence weakens the group's objectivity and creativity. Chronic anxiety embeds itself in the very fabric of the relationship, becoming a part of the nature of the system itself. What seems trivial to someone from the outside triggers the anxious behavior on the inside.

Chronically anxious members will act out their anxiety in an attempt to get relief, all of which is highly dysfunctional to personal relationships and to the congregation (e.g., spreading rumors, making accusations, exaggerating events).

Even if the conditions are changed or the issue resolved, dysfunctional people will find another issue to feed their anxiety, and they will attempt to displace their anxiety on others. When others take up their anxiety and begin to "act out," the dysfunctional people relax. Now they don't have to be anxious because the pastor, board, or some other group is carrying the anxiety. This becomes a vicious cycle of 1) be anxious; 2) make others anxious; 3) rest awhile; and 4) be anxious again.

Another indicator of extreme dysfunction is the denial that any anxiety exists. Now, instead of being overly concerned, the people deny any existence of anxiety. They claim everyone is together in a kind of perpetual love-in: "We're all one big happy family. Everyone loves one another. Everything is just fine. What a close group we are!" In fact, they are not a close group with appropriate boundaries, they are a *stuck together* group.

Their denial of reality produces a blindness to the true condition, so that persons are no longer able to recognize their unconscious destructive patterns. They are totally oblivious to the fact that they are acting in a dysfunctional manner.

Anxiety in a healthy congregation

Healthy congregations may also experience anxiety. For example, a major change or loss that takes people by surprise can trigger anxiety. A petition circulated to remove the pastor, a church leader who suffers a moral crisis, or a key family leaving the church may be the triggering event that raises the anxiety level within a congregation.

However, in a healthy congregation anxiety, when it is brought to light and addressed, can be the motivation to correct problems, make necessary changes or work out relational differences.

Anxiety provokes change. It prods and pushes us toward innovation or transformation. If, however, it reaches a certain intensity, it prevents the very change it provokes. What was stimulus becomes restraint. We "lose our head" or "cool." Essentially what is lost is our awareness and composure; we are too reactive to be responsive.

Anxiety is a warning signal to the congregation that there is some threat, some need that must be addressed. This is *acute* anxiety that is situational and "time-based." The healthy congregation will acknowledge the situation and address it so that, in due time, the anxiety is abated. *Chronic* anxiety, however, is a habitual condition that never ends.

DEBILITATING PERSONAL BOUNDARIES

Boundaries help persons know themselves and others. In human relationships persons need to be separate and to be close; They need to be alone and to be together. No one defines this reality more poignantly than Dietrich Bonhoeffer, who became a martyr for the faith at the end of World War II:

> ... only as we are in fellowship can we be alone, and only he [or she] that is alone can live in fellowship.... Each by itself has profound pitfalls and perils. One who wants fellowship without solitude plunges into the void of words and feelings, and one who seeks solitude without fellowship perishes in the abyss of vanity, self-infatuation and despair.[2]

For healthy persons, boundaries help people to know how close they want to be in relationship with others, whether they wish to be intimate or remain at a greater distance. Likewise, boundaries also helps people to know how much they wish to be alone, and to what extent they wish to be with others.

Dysfunction in one's personal boundaries may take one of two possible expressions: one possibility is to have no boundaries at all so that the person can never stand to be alone, or is unable to think or act independently. The second possibility is for the person to cut oneself off from others, allowing no one to get near, or to penetrate his or her tightly fortified exterior.

Persons who have no boundaries

In the church, persons who subvert their own interdependence because of their need to stick to others become 'meeting freaks' or addictive volunteers. On the other hand, they never have time for solitary prayer or reflection, no time to be silent before God. These people become perennial groupies who must always have a company around them. If they find themselves alone for a single moment they either are overwhelmed with lonesomeness, or they suffer anxiety attacks.

Persons who become highly anxious about being alone become "clinging vines," clutching at relationships. When there are such people in the church, they eventually find one another. Their boundaries become so enmeshed that they are unable to think or feel without taking cues from those to whom they cling. Instead of touching others' lives, they clutch them. They have no thoughts other than the group's thoughts, no opinion other than the group's opinion.

When any one moves in a certain direction, they all move in that direction. This is the *series relationship* pattern we discussed earlier. People become stuck together because they draw their 'energy' and 'breath' from these dysfunctional, symbiotic relationships.

People who have very rigid boundaries

On the other side of the ledger are persons who cut themselves off from all relationships with others. Being anxious about being close, they relate only from an emotional distance. Cut off from feelings, they can have no empathy for others' feelings. Such persons function by avoiding relationships or overtly battling them.

Such people often exert tremendous influence upon the church by reason of their refusal to share what they are thinking, so that every one is left guessing what they want. They often want a position in the church, but will run the show all by themselves.

BOUNDARIES AND OVERFUNCTIONING

As the leader of a large congregation, Moses once complained to God:

> *"Where am I to get meat to give to all this people? For they come weeping to me and say, 'Give us meat to eat!' I am not able to carry all this people alone, for they are too heavy for me. If this is the way you are going to treat me, put me to death at once..." (Numbers 11:13-15a)*

This must have been one of Moses' more dysfunctional moments.

What we observe in Moses' behavior is *overfunctioning.* Overfunctioning seems to be a characteristic almost unique to anxious pastors, and other codependents.

Overfunctioning is the condition of assuming an unhealthy responsibility for the way others function and for the quality of their relationships — and then becoming anxious when they still don't act as we think they should. Taking on responsibility for certain members or the entire congregation is a setup that draws out the dark and lonely side of the leader — frustration, discouragement, anxiety, lack of spiritual vitality and even suicide prayers, as seen in Moses' prayer, above.

Sooner or later, overfunctioning will cause the pastor and key lay leaders to lead from the underbelly of their anxiety, compulsions and fears. Overfunctioning will ultimately cause the leaders to lead from the dark side of their personalities. The darksome expressions of leadership can be characterized as: suspicious, compulsive, detached, dramatic, depressed leadership.[3] Whenever the leader leads from the dark side, the congregation will come to reflect, exhibit the leader's neuroses. Thus dysfunction breeds greater dysfunction.

Clergy who overfunction take on the responsibility for the feelings, thoughts and spirituality of others while giving to others the responsibility for his own feelings, thoughts and spirituality. Overfunctioning is one way of managing anxiety and handling relationships under stress. For some, overfunctioning is a reaction in their attempts to lift another person's spirits or to convince others of exactly what they need to do.

In the literature on leadership, Jesus is consistently put forth as one of the greatest leaders in history. What is it about Jesus that is so appealing to historians and leaders? For one thing, he never overfunctioned. He walked around a lot, he prayed a lot, he enjoyed a good meal, he gave good straight-forward advice. But he never took pains to check up on people to be sure they were heeding his counsel, and he didn't get out of sorts when they chose otherwise. His leadership was: 1) establish a friendship, 2) challenge their damaging behavior, and 3) leave them alone to decide their response.

While many leaders complain that a congregation's members are not being responsible enough, they will continue to reinforce the pattern by taking the responsibility upon themselves. Often a relationship of unhealthy dependence is developed with leaders who exhibit slave or martyr type leader behaviors.[4] Overfunctioners and underfunctioners reinforce each other in a circular fashion, and it takes a strong decision by at least one of the players to stop the destructive pattern.

In his prayer, Moses finally came to a vulnerable state, expressing his honest feelings to God. This is hard for overfunctioners who have difficulty sharing their own vulnerability with others — they seem to always know what is best for others as much as for themselves, moving in quickly to advise and rescue others. They also have difficulty allowing others to struggle with their own problems. The spiritual effect of overfunctioning is portentous. In subtle yet profound ways, overfunctioning depletes the interior life of the leader. For the overfunctioner, everything hinges on controlling the other person. The challenge for the overfunctioning person is to learn how to take *more* responsibility for his or her own self and *less* responsibility for the thoughts, feelings and behaviors of others.

RUNAWAY EMOTIONS

People construct their emotional boundaries while they are yet children. As children, they observe how the older members of the family express or repress emotions, and from this they take their cues of how emotions are to be managed. Further, people whose emotions were severely wounded when they were children, due to such traumatic events as physical abuse, sexual molestation, violence in the household, will tend to express emotions either by great explosions of anger, or by turning the anger in upon themselves. For such persons, emotions and how they are expressed, have to do with survival.

When emotionally damaged children grow up they will either work out their emotions by becoming sexual abusers or otherwise violent people; or they will internalize their 'frightening and dangerous' emotions by building closed, rigid boundaries around themselves; or they will become codependent, hoping to placate the addict and, thus, reduce the fear and anxiety in their own lives.

When emotionally damaged people come into the church, they bring their hurt, fear, anger, rage with them. Unless these persons are healed, they are prime candidates for joining into series relationships, becoming a timid, or an antagonistic loner, filling codependent roles for addictive persons or processes in the congregation, or they will seek an identified patient upon whom they may transfer their own symptoms.

This last possibility is especially telling for pastors (or spouses) since they will often join the congregation as a loving, 'willing to do anything for the pastor,' only to later blame him or her for all of the problems they are experiencing in their lives. Now their search for an identified patient to carry their symptoms is complete.

EMOTIONAL TRIANGLES

It takes three to triangle. When two parties in a dysfunctional relationship become uncomfortable with one another, the most anxious of them will "triangle in" a third party. Shifting the focus to a third party lowers the anxiety of the two persons in the original relationship. The two persons become anxious about the third party's behavior, and are no longer anxious about each other's behavior.

Triangles come in many forms. The third party need not always be a person. Often times the third party is a concern or issue. *A person is "triangled" in when he or she is caught in the middle — as the focus of an unresolved issue.* The intent of the emotional triangle is to finally have the third party carry all of the pent-up anxiety on behalf of the others. Thus, the third party becomes the symptom bearer of the others' anxiety. The symptom bearer ends up carrying the anxiety for the others, who are then free to go their own ways, feeling less anxious and less responsible for the situation that caused the anxiety in the first place.

In a congregation, gossip is a universal form of triangulation that focuses on the faults of a third party and, therefore, takes the focus off the persons engaged in the gossip conversation. The higher the anxiety, the more likely people will be to triangle a third party whom they hope will be blamed for the problem. All of this is often carried out along a gossip trail or by "passing the buck," until a symptom bearer is discovered who can not pass the buck any further, and so becomes the personification of the others' anxiety.

For example, the story of anxious Adam who, upon being confronted by God, triangled Eve into the relationship. Being brought into this triangle caused Eve a good deal of anxiety. So in her anxious response, Eve blames the Serpent. This, of course, created another triangle: God, Eve and the Serpent.

The more enmeshed people are in their relationships within a congregation, the greater the number and intensity of triangles. A real life example of triangles follows, to demonstrate how emotional triangles are generated:

A pastor was called to serve a small congregation of about forty members. Within the first week of his arrival the church's piano player visited the pastor to report that the choir director was spreading rumors around town that the piano player (a married woman) was having an affair. The piano player reasoned that the rumors had done so much damage to her reputation in the congregation that she would have to give up her position as piano player. She also stated that there was no one else in the congregation who could play the piano.

This made the pastor quite anxious. He begged her not to resign, and said that he would have a visit with the choir director. When he asked the choir director why she was spreading such rumors about the piano player, the choir director retorted that she and the piano player were best friends, that she never said such a thing about the piano player, and she knew the piano player would never say such horrible things about her. Now the pastor was caught between the two different positions of the women. This episode filled out the first emotional triangle:

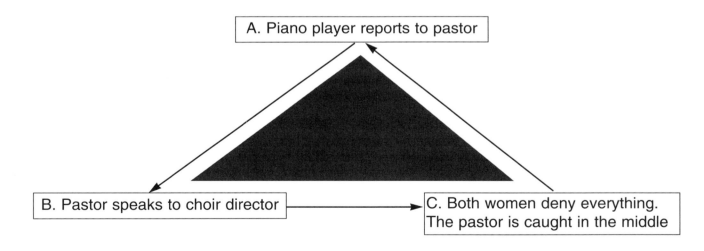

A. Piano player reports to pastor

B. Pastor speaks to choir director

C. Both women deny everything. The pastor is caught in the middle

Then both of the women reported to the church board that the new pastor was trying to destroy their friendship by spreading vicious rumors about both of them. This made the board highly anxious. The board met with the pastor. The pastor asked to meet with the board and the two women. This episode led to the second emotional triangle:

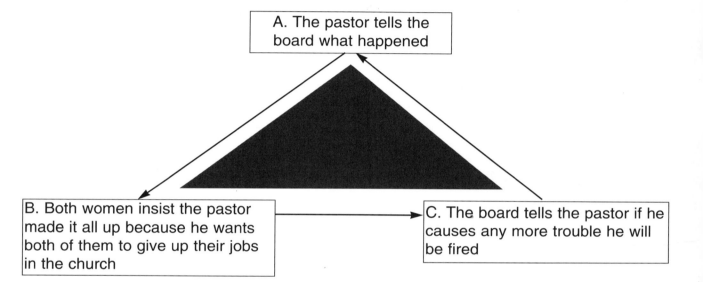

The story illustrates that emotional triangles spin off one after another, causing a web of highly anxious and emotional relationships. The story also illustrates how *stuck together* people can actually become in a dysfunctional congregation. The two women were stuck to each other. Further, the board was stuck to the two women, so that its members were unable to remain neutral in the situation, and thus were unable to work through the emotions to arrive at truth. The story also illustrates how quickly this dysfunctional congregation succeeded in making its new pastor its identified patient, its symptom bearer.

Earlier in this chapter it was said that the third party in a triangle might be a condition. Figure 3.2 illustrates this principle. The diagram also illustrates how triangles spin off of one another, creating a web of triangles:

Figure 3.2

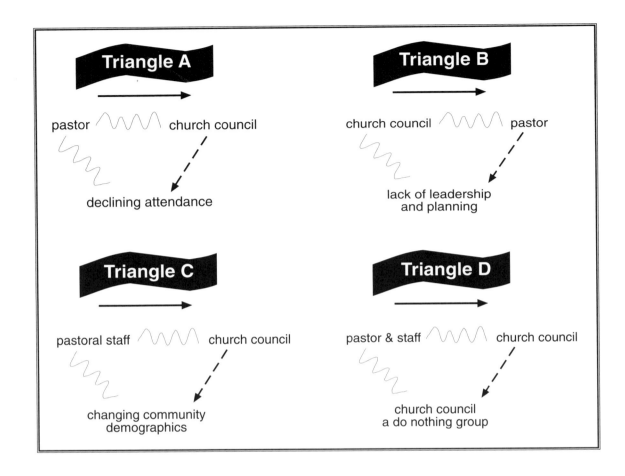

In triangle A, the pastor is experiencing anxiety over declining attendance, attempts to bring the church board into a triangle so that he need not feel anxious alone. In response, several board members suggest that the problem may be due to a lack of leadership and planning on the part of the pastor and clergy staff (triangle B). The pastor shared the board's opinion with the staff, who attempts to shift the burden to the changing complexion of the community (triangle C). Further, the clergy staff asks to meet with the board to discuss the matter. The meeting of the board and staff brought accusations and counter accusations. The staff finally suggests that the real problem lies with the board's unwillingness to become involved in hands-on ministry in the community (triangle D).

In these web triangles we see pastor, staff and board all attempting to make the other party(s) the identified patient. Episodes such as these occur thousands of times every week, as

notes notes

pastors and board members attempt to shift the burden of failed expectations onto one another. As a result the anxiety creeps into the congregations, hundreds of pastors are fired or resign, board members resign, and congregation's cycle into conflict — every week.

PARALYZING HOMEOSTASIS

Homeostasis comprises the habitual response patterns which the congregation uses as self-correcting mechanisms to keep everything on 'balance,' in order to preserve its existence, "as is." The maintenance of the congregation's stability or equilibrium, may be healthy or destructive. Nevertheless, every congregation that survives over time has its homeostatic principles, implicit or explicit, that tends to adjust toward a desired balance, its homeostasis.

Homeostasis in a healthy congregation

In a healthy congregation, homeostasis is good and necessary. Homeostatic conditions are habitual, and a congregation needs healthy habits. Habits conserve much time and energy. Without habits the congregation would be in a constant state of uncertainty. It would never know what to expect next. Pastors are in the habit of preparing for the Sunday services. Members are in the habit of going to church on Sunday, and putting their offerings in the offering plate.

Without these habits the pastor might forget, or too long delay, to prepare for the next Sunday. Other urgent matters might eat up his or her time; and the members would have to think through every Sunday whether to go to church, or lounge around at home with the Sunday newspaper, a cup of coffee, and some Dunkin' Donuts.

All of the habits, routines and relationships that surround a healthy church combine to create its homeostasis.

A dysfunctional congregation also has its habits, many of which frustrate all efforts to build a vital congregation. The antagonistic member is in the habit of trying to get on the church board or to hold some position of influence — so that he or she might "set things right" in the church. When many such forces converge, they create a homeostatic condition that is deadly. Unhealthy homeostatic habits, when they converge, exert tremendous forces that hinder change when the congregation is stuck in an undesirable condition.

The cases presented in Chapters 1 and 2 illustrate that unhealthy congregations will stick together to their own detriment:

> *In work systems, the stabilizing effect of the identified patient and the resistance from the togetherness at all costs help explain why even the most ruthless corporation (no less churches and synagogues) often will tolerate and adapt to trouble-making complainers and down right incompetents, whereas the creative thinkers who disturb the balance of things will be ignored, or let go.[5]*

The emotional climate of a dysfunctional congregation is highly volatile. It seems the congregation might 'self destruct' at any moment. But it does not. People stay together in the midst of tremendous pressure and pain. What keeps the members from leaving, or flying apart in every direction? The group's homeostasis holds it together. And an interesting homeostatic condition it is. The dysfunctional members are in the habit of igniting one conflict after another, and the more healthy members are in the habit of letting them do it.

> *[Whenever a particular issue] ... won't go away despite numerous, reasonable efforts to compromise with the more vociferous, then the issues under dispute are not the issues. ... the underlying homeostatic forces are sometimes more difficult to identify because they tend to be camouflaged in religious terminology[6]*

An example of an homeostatic condition within a congregation might be taken from the functioning of its official board. The 'thermostat' that maintains the 'temperature' of the board's interpersonal and intergroup relationships does not maintain the temperature at a fixed point. Rather, it controls the temperature within an acceptable range. For example, during a church board meeting, the pastor may "turn up the thermostat" on an issue which the board is discussing. And immediately, or soon thereafter, a board member will "turn it down."

The board is comfortable when the 'temperature' within their relationships remain within a fixed range. However, when the emotional climate climbs above, or falls below, the acceptable range, everyone in the room senses tension, anxiety, anger or fear because the homeostasis of the board has been disrupted. Efforts to regain homeostasis might include an attempt to balance power, relieve pain and discomfort, to introduce humor or to motivate others to action.

Dysfunctional persons in the congregation seem to possess unusual skill in upsetting the congregation's stability. For example, the board adopts a plan to solve a particular problem. Everyone thinks the issue has been resolved. However, after a few days or months, it surfaces again, and the board cycles back to where it was before – to spend endless hours haggling over the problem that appeared to be resolved. Thus, a board or congregation may cycle around the same problem again and again spending endless hours and much energy and get nowhere – allowing a dysfunctional member or group to set the agenda for the church for months or years.

Changes that affect a congregation's homeostasis

There are many conditions that may upset the homeostatic condition of a congregation. A brief list of the major conditions follows:

1. Changes in the spiritual leader (pastor or lay person):
   a. Birth, death, illness, divorce, extra-marital affair, need for psychotherapy for the pastor or spouse.

   b. Professional advancement in the life of the pastor: studying for a new degree, dedicated involvement in a community project, committee involvement in the denomination.

2. Changes in the long-term key lay leaders:
   The family who has 'run the church' for decades moves away, extra-marital affair, divorce, death, a new spiritual experience.

3. Changes in the community:
   Racial, average age, economy, decline in population, rapid growth in population.

4. Changes in the congregation's staff:
   Hiring, firing, or resignation of a key employee (especially the church secretary, or volunteer finance secretary).

5. Changes in the denomination:
   Decline, restructuring, supporting unpopular issues, increase in costs levied on the congregation.

6. Changes in the ministry results:
   a. Dramatic decline in membership, lack of quality conscious volunteers, insufficient funds to launch new ministries.

   b. Dramatic and unexpected ministry success, influx of new members, gaining public attention, new pastor.[7]

While any one of these issues does not necessarily cause problems, a convergence of these conditions is able to contribute to increased congregation anxiety. This helps to explain how a particular issue may have certain consequences at one time and very different consequences at another time.

These, then, are the results of dysfunction in the congregation: fever-pitch anxiety, debilitating personal boundaries, runaway emotions, emotional triangles and paralyzing homeostasis. It is important to remember that, *with the exception of emotional triangles*, each of these processes is functional in a healthy congregation. Problems arise when they reach a 'spin out' point. Then the processes, themselves, become the agenda for the dysfunctional persons in the congregation.

This concludes our study of the causes and results of dysfunction in a congregation. We will now proceed to a review of this material and, finally, a study of the more effective means for intervening in the processes of a dysfunctional congregation. First, however, it is time for your mental digestion of the materials covered in this chapter.

TIME OUT
FOR A MENTAL DIGESTION

1. List the results of dysfunction and describe them. After you have recalled all you can from memory, check the text to fill in the items you missed.
2. Where in your church do you observe these results? In your family? In yourself?
3. List the leadership styles that grow out of overfunctioning, out of the 'dark side'. After you have recalled all you can from memory, check the text to fill in the items you missed.
4. Are you overfunctioning in any area of your leadership? Are you leading out of the dark side? If so, what type of darksome leadership are you utilizing?
3. Develop some concrete plans for reducing or eliminating these results: What will you do? When will you do it? With whom will you do it? What results do you expect to accomplish?

[1] For a more complete study of conflict in the congregation, see Norman Shawchuck and Roger Heuser, *Managing the Congregation: Building Effective Systems to Serve People* (Nashville: Abingdon Press, 1993), pp.245 - 313.

[2] Dietrich Bonhoffer, *Life Together* (New York: Harper & Row, 1954).

[3] For a study of the dark side of leadership, see Norman Shawchuck and Roger Heuser, *Leading the Congregation: Caring for Yourself While Serving the People* (Nashville: Abingdon Press, 1993), pp. 94-107.

[4] The martyr leader attempts to maintain control over others by producing feelings of guilt and/or pity. The slave leader maintains a sense of worthlessness or guilt unless constantly occupied by some activity. The slave tries to assuage guilt; the martyr causes it. For more discussion of the slave and martyr leadership style in religious organizations, see Norman Shawchuck, *How To Be A More Effective Church Leader* (Leith, North Dakota: Spiritual Growth Resources, 1990), pp. 26-27.

[5] Edwin H. Friedman, *Generation to Generation: Family Process in Church and Synagogue*, p.25.

[6] Michael H. Crosby, *The Dysfunctional Church: Addiction and Codependency in the Family of Catholocism*, p.28.

[7] Some of these conditions were borrowed from Edwin H. Friedman, *Generation to Generation: Family process in Church and Synagogue*, pp. 203-204.

GREAT

resources

CHAPTER 1: INTRODUCING FAMILY SYSTEMS THEORY AND ORGANIZATIONAL DYSFUNCTION

FAMILY SYSTEMS THEORY

notes ● notes

Family Systems Theory is a new science that seeks to explain the causes of increasing family stress and breakdown in American society. The theory goes on to describe the types of interventions that are most effective in turning back the symptoms of this dysfunction.

Family Systems Theory is appropriate for intervening into relational breakdown in congregations, because a congregation behaves like a family. The members of a congregation relate more as a family than a highly structured organization or institution.

When a family is under stress or not meeting the needs of its members, the anxiety does not occur solely because of one person. Stress and anxiety are a family affair. Therefore, in order to understand the behaviors of individual family members, it is important to see how persons function in their family contexts.

The five basic principles of family systems theory

There are five principles that form the foundation for family systems theory, as it might be applied to congregations. These principles form the foundation for working with a congregation in conflict:

1. The congregation as a whole is greater than the sum of its parts.
2. If you change one part of the congregation system, you change the whole congregation.
3. Systems become more complex and organized over time.
4. The congregation is open, changing, goal directive and adaptive.
5. Individual dysfunction is a reflection of an active emotional system.

DYSFUNCTIONAL CONGREGATIONS

When persons not so socially or psychologically well adapted become members of a congregation they bring their maladjustments with them. If they are not healed in the church, sooner or later they will almost certainly become a cause of conflict which reflects their own internal disappointments with life. This type of world-view is termed 'dysfunctional.' In such situations an entirely new body of theory and interventions are needed, because dysfunctional people play by an entirely different set of rules when they are in conflict.

There are four guiding principles which help us understand the possible extent of dysfunction in the congregation, or in a member's life:

1. Persons who are competent in all other areas of their lives may be dysfunctional in the church
2. Often a relatively small group is dysfunctional in a church, with the rest of the people being competent
3. An entire congregation can become dysfunctional
4. Dysfunction in a congregation is often passed on from generation to generation.

Dysfunction in the congregation is to be measured more by degrees than fixed stages. If a congregation were 100% dysfunctional it could not long survive, since it would have no means by which to carry on any of its functions.

How dysfunction enters the congregation

Dysfunction enters the congregation through the life experiences of its members. When dysfunctional people enter the congregation, or when members experience chronic anxiety, this has its effect upon the congregation.

Dysfunctional persons make entrance into a congregation through a number of avenues, such as:

1. The congregation hires a new pastor who is dysfunctional
2. Persons become new members who are dysfunctional
3. Over time members experience a series of events which can move people toward dysfunction. Somewhere along the way a once healthy person moves toward dysfunction.

CHAPTER 2: THE BUILDING BLOCKS OF A DYS- FUNCTIONAL CONGREGATION

Congregations do not become dysfunctional for no reason, nor do they become dysfunctional over night. A number of relational conditions must converge to move a congregation to dysfunction. These conditions are:

ADDICTIVE BEHAVIOR

An addiction is any **substance** or **process** that has taken over our lives and over which we are powerless. It may not be a physiological addiction. Anything can become addictive.

Addictions can be formed from the abuse of *chemicals* (i.e., drugs, alcohol, nicotine, caffeine)or the abuse of processes:(i.e., religion, sex, money, work, conflict, power).

Process addictions serve the same function as a chemical or substance addiction. The addiction serves to alter the mood of the individual or group so that they might escape unwanted feelings and/or anxiety.

COMPULSIVE BEHAVIOR

Compulsion is a special form of process addiction. It is characterized by workaholism, perfectionism, the insistence that others submit to one's way of doing things.

CODEPENDENT BEHAVIOR

Addictive relationships must have at least two parties to play out the dysfunction: the addict and the codependent. The addict uses a substance or process to escape from his or her unwanted feelings. The codependent stabilizes the situation so it doesn't collapse. Every addict needs a codependent in order to survive. Every codependent needs an addict in order to feel worthwhile.

In the final analysis there is no difference between the results of addiction or codependency. Both the addict and the codependent are addicted. The addict is addicted to the addictive process or substance. The codependent is addicted to the process of protecting the addict.

IDENTIFIED PATIENT (SYMPTOM BEARER)

When a congregation comes under serious stress, it often will try to transfer its anxiety upon a person or group; which becomes the identified patient (the symptom bearer) for the congregation. The symptom bearer is not necessarily the "sick" member of the congregation. The congregation-as-a-whole is the carrier of the illness. Keeping the focus on a "problem" person or group prevents the congregation from addressing the systemic issues that contributed to the symptoms in the first place.

SERIES RELATIONSHIPS

A series relationship occurs when persons cannot act independently of one another. People in a series relationship are not *together* so much as they are *stuck together*. Whatever one person in this *stuck together* group thinks or does, all the other people in the group will think or do, since they have no capacity to think critically about the behavior of the person who is setting the agenda.

As a stuck together group they can act in ways that paralyze the rest of the congregation. They often succeed in becoming a powerful, influential block that sets the agenda for the congregation for years on end. In this condition the dysfunctional group acts as the addictive party, while the rest of the congregation plays the codependent role. Often the people in the congregation are totally oblivious to the fact that it is their codependent behavior which makes it possible for the dysfunctional group to continue.

CHAPTER 3: THE RESULTS OF DYSFUNCTION IN THE CONGREGATION

The results of dysfunctional conflict in a congregation are:

ANXIETY

In a dysfunctional congregation anxieties run at a high pitch. Always a person or group is gripped with anxiety, and fears the absolute worst is going to fall upon the congregation.

Chronically anxious members will act out their anxiety in an attempt to get relief, (e.g., spreading rumors, making accusations, exaggerating events). This is done in an attempt to displace their anxiety on others. When others take up their anxiety and begin to "act out," the dysfunctional people relax. They don't have to be anxious because the pastor, board, or some other group is carrying the anxiety. This becomes a vicious cycle of 1) be anxious; 2) make others anxious; 3) rest awhile; and 4) be anxious again.

BOUNDARIES

Dysfunction in one's personal boundaries may take one of two possible expressions. One possibility is to have no boundaries. The second possibility is to have highly rigid boundaries.

Persons who have no boundaries

Persons who subvert their own interdependence become 'meeting freaks' or addictive volunteers. They become perennial groupies who must always have a company around them. If they find themselves alone for a single moment they are overwhelmed with lonesomeness or suffer anxiety attacks. Instead of touching others' lives, they clutch them. They have no thoughts other than the group's thoughts, no opinion other than the group's opinion.

People who have very rigid boundaries

People who have very rigid boundaries cut themselves off from all relationships with others. Such people often exert tremendous influence upon the church by reason of their refusal to share what he is thinking, so that every one is left guessing what he wants.

Boundaries and overfunctioning

Overfunctioning is the condition of assuming an unhealthy responsibility for the way others function and for the quality of their relationships. Sooner or later, overfunctioning will cause the pastor and key lay leaders to lead from the under-belly of their anxiety, compulsions and fears.

The darksome expressions of leadership can be characterized as: suspicious, compulsive, detached, dramatic, depressed leadership. Whenever the leader leads from the dark side, the congregation will come to reflect, exhibit the leader's neuroses.

EMOTIONS

People whose emotions were severely wounded when they were children will tend to express emotions either by great explosions of anger, or by turning the anger in upon themselves. As children they learned that this is what they must do to survive.

When emotionally damaged people come into the church, they bring their hurt, fear, anger and rage with them. Unless these persons are healed, they are prime candidates for joining into series relationships, becoming a timid, or an antagonistic loner, filling codependent roles for addictive persons or processes in the congregation, or they will seek an identified patient upon whom they may transfer their own symptoms.

TRIANGLES

When two parties in a dysfunctional relationship become uncomfortable with one another, the most anxious of them will "triangle in" a third party. Shifting the focus to a third party lowers the anxiety of the two persons in the original relationship. The two persons become anxious about the third party's behavior, and are no longer anxious about each other's behavior.

Triangles come in many forms. The third party need not always be a person. Often times the third party is a concern or issue. The intent of the emotional triangle is to finally have the third party carry all of the pent-up anxiety on behalf of the others. Thus, the third party becomes the symptom bearer of the others' anxiety.

HOMEOSTASIS

Homeostasis comprises the habitual response patterns which the congregation uses as self-correcting mechanisms to keep everything on 'balance,' in order to preserve its existence, "as is." The maintenance of the congregation's stability or equilibrium, may be healthy or destructive. A dysfunctional congregation creates habits for itself that constantly keep it in a homeostatic condition which ensures that nothing will change.

Changes that affect a congregation's homeostasis

There are many conditions that may upset the homeostatic condition of a congregation:

1. Changes in the spiritual leader (pastor or lay person)
2. Changes in the long-term key lay leaders
3. Changes in the community
4. Changes in the congregation's staff
5. Changes in the denomination
6. Changes in the ministry results.

While any one of these issues does not necessarily cause problems, a convergence of these conditions is able to contribute to increased congregation anxiety.

With this brief review, we will now proceed to an in-depth study of the intervention methods which tend to prove most effective in dealing with dysfunctional persons and groups.

CHAPTER 5

INTERVENING IN DYSFUNCTIONAL CONFLICTS

When the congregation is a healthy system, individual members thrive because of the empowering influence of the life of the body. When the congregation is unhealthy, our efforts to equip a few motivated individuals are usually doomed.[2]

• R. Paul Stevens and Phil Collins

When dealing with a conflict that grows out of dysfunctional relationships in the congregation, as compared to normal conflict, all the rules change. The theories and processes that work well in normal conflict situations do not work in dysfunctional settings. Dysfunction calls for a different approach.

INTRODUCTION TO INTERVENTION THEORY

There are two ways of changing an organization: intervention and accident. An intervention is a specific plan of action, with defined anticipated results. This is different from an accident. An accident is not planned. Even though it may produce good results, it was neither defined nor anticipated.[3]

Chris Argyris states that there are two types of organizations, Model I and Model II, each of which utilizes its unique intervention strategies. He terms these two types: model I and model II organizations. He describes the operational values of each as follows:[4]

MODEL I ORGANIZATION

Operating assumptions:

1. **Work to achieve the goals that I want for the organization:**
    In a Model I organization, every one is working to make this happen.

2. **In every situation, seek to win and never lose:**
    In a Model I organization, every one is committed to always having his or her own way. To compromise seems like a personal loss or failure.

3. **Avoid emotions and open conflict at every cost:**
    Model I organizations feel that emotions are a sign of character weakness and conflict and disagreements are to be kept under cover.

4. **Be rational:**
    Model I organizations distrust intuition, hunches, dreams.
    Emotions are downplayed as being immature. Only rationality is trusted.

MODEL II ORGANIZATION

Operating assumptions:

1. **Generate valid and useful information:**
    Model II organizations know that no positive change can happen unless all of the parties involved have valid information to work with — presented in a useful form. The information must be given to them in ways that they can fully understand.

2. **Allow free and informed choice:**
    People must be allowed to make choices/decisions freely. However, only good information will allow them to make informed choices. In a modern society only choices that are free and informed will change things.[5]

3. **Motivate commitment to the choices that are made:**
    After the decisions are made, people must be helped to remain committed to them. The process of following these three steps is, itself, a means of motivating commitment. The process keeps people involved, and people support what they help create.

Argyris finds 95% of all American organizations (including religious) operate by the model I principles. Only 5% operate by the model II principles.

For the purposes of this discussion on intervention, the most important consideration from Argyris' teaching is that *interventions can be planned and carried out as either Model I interventions, or Model II interventions.*[6]

Model I interventions never affect positive change, and most certainly not in dysfunctional settings. However, given the volatility of the dysfunctional congregation, the temptation is to use Model I interventions. This temptation must be avoided at every cost. Only Model II interventions will work in the church, and most certainly in dysfunctional settings.

The three elements of intervention

In their book, *Consultation,*[7] Robert Blake and Jane Mouton observe that intervention planning must be done around three considerations:

1. What unit of change will be the focus of the intervention: individual, group, intergroup, total organization?

2. What are the focal issues of the conflict: power & authority, morale & cohesion, norms & standards, goals & objectives?

3. (Based upon considerations 1 & 2) What type of intervention will be utilized: theory & principles, prescriptive, confrontation, catalytic, acceptant?

LEVELS OF ADDICTION IN THE CHURCH

There are four possible levels of addiction in an organization. The levels progressively increase in complexity. [8]

1. *A first level addiction in a congregation is one in which a key person is an addict.* This may be the pastor, a key lay leader, or a highly influential member. Anne Wilson Shaef illustrates this pattern through the words of an adult daughter regarding her father, a pastor whose workaholic addictions killed him:

> *His work was the most important thing in our family. If any of us complained about never seeing him, he always had the excuse that he was doing 'the Lord's work' and working himself to death was justified. ... Although he was always working on the run, his actual productivity decreased. He recycled old sermons more and more often. He died in his late 40's and no one ever knew him. I feel like I had a nonrecovering alcoholic for a father. He did not really serve Christ or the church. I now know he served his disease.[9]*

2. *A second level addiction is when individuals join the congregation and bring their dysfunction with them.* This may be a person who becomes a member, or a group that joins the congregation, often as the result of a split in another church.

3. *A third level addiction is when the congregation-as-a-whole functions like an addictive substance; the organization itself provides the "fix."* The church functions as an addictive substance when the members become hooked on the services and promises of the church — and ignore how the entire system is really operating; often denying or overlooking warning signs of dysfunction and breakdown.

4. *A fourth level of addiction is when the congregation itself becomes an addict.* In this instance the dysfunction of several members finally invades the behavior of the entire congregation. Communications become indirect, not open, not honest. Emotional triangles continually spring up. Gossip runs rampant. The leaders and workers become skilled in incompetence, and finally all the systems cease to function in a healthy or effective manner.

This ends our crash course in intervention theory. We will now proceed to consider the more effective interventions in the behaviors of dysfunctional congregations.

RULES FOR WORKING IN A DYSFUNCTIONAL CONGREGATION

The following intervention strategies may seem to be easy when we read about them. However, they are not easy in the context of real-life dysfunction. Nonetheless, to heal dysfunctional persons or congregations, there are no alternatives.

1. BE A NON-ANXIOUS PRESENCE

In a dysfunctional setting anxiety is everywhere present. There is little reprieve. When these conditions prevail long enough, it is possible even for the healthy members and leaders to be caught up in the anxiety.

However, when one gets caught up in the system's anxiety, he or she becomes a bearer of the illness and is no longer able to bring health to those who are not healthy. It is easier to say this than it is to be remain non-anxious in the presence of anxiety. Nonetheless, *the interventionist must remain outside of the anxiety.* No one makes this point more compellingly than Edwin Friedman:

> *The capacity of members of the clergy to contain their own anxiety regarding congregational matters, both those not related to them as well as those where they become the identified focus, may be the most significant capability in their arsenal ... because of the systemic effect that a leader's functioning always has on an entire [congregation]. A nonanxious presence will modify anxiety throughout the entire congregation..*[10]

To *remain connected to the people who are anxious, while not becoming anxious*, is the most significant intervention capability the pastor and leaders can develop.

2. UTILIZE PLAYFULNESS

Only the people who are non-anxious can be playful in the midst of much anxiety. Anxiety always sets a tone of utter seriousness. The best antidote for stifling, draining seriousness is playfulness. Of this Friedman says, "*The capacity of clergy to be paradoxical, challenging (rather than saving), earthy, sometimes crazy, and even "devilish," often can do more to loosen knots in a congregational relationship than the most well-meaning "serious efforts.*"[11]

3. STAY OUT OF EMOTIONAL TRIANGLES

People who remain non-anxious are better able to spot triangles, because they are not caught up in the anxiety and runaway emotions that are going on in the triangle. However, even with your most vigilant effort, you will likely be triangled from time to time.

The harm is not in getting triangled, but in staying in the triangle. When you discover that you are caught in a triangle, immediately bring the two parties together and tell them that you are 'triangled' into their problem, and that you are stepping out of the triangle. Also ask whether you might help them to live free of triangles in the future.

If remaining non-anxious is the leader's first line of offense in dysfunction, staying out of emotional triangles is the second.

4. WITHDRAW SUPPORT FROM SERIES RELATIONSHIPS

Coach the healthy members to recognize series relationships, to understand their negative effects upon those who are in them, and upon the life and work of the congregation.

When you see people who are trying to break out of a series relationship, make every effort to support them. Getting out of a series relationship is never easy. All the others in the relationship exert great pressure to keep the person with them, almost as if their life depends up the person staying in. And to some extent this is true, because when someone breaks the series chain, several others are cut off from the energy source that is feeding the dysfunctional relationship.

A common characteristic in dysfunctional congregations is that one person or a group will succeed in setting the board's agenda for months or years; and the essential work of the board never gets done. All positive efforts grind to a halt. These people are antagonists.

Antagonists are individuals, who on the basis of nonsubstantive evidence, go out of their way to make insatiable demands, usually attacking the person or performance of others. These attacks are selfish in nature, tearing down rather than building up, and are frequently directed against those in a leadership capacity.[12]

Interventions needed in this instance must be focused upon the board and other key leaders; training, raising awareness, coaching.

5. COACH THE HEALTHIEST MEMBERS OF THE CONGREGATION

Coach the healthiest members of the congregation to break the dysfunctional dynamics going on in the church. Do not try to heal the congregation by placing primary attention upon the dysfunctional members. This is an important principle and it stresses something absolutely opposite from other intervention disciplines.

This principle is based upon the premise that, in an addictive congregation or family, only the family can heal the family. However, the most severely dysfunctional in the family (addict, codependent, identified patient, those locked into series relationships) lack the internal resources to heal themselves, let alone the rest of the family. So you begin where the greatest health is. You coach the most healthy to take the steps that are necessary for the healing of the congregation.

6. RELATE TO EVERYONE OPENLY AND HONESTLY

This item is one of the most difficult to live up to, and one that will bite you the hardest if you don't.

Working with a dysfunctional congregation gives you no good place to begin a healing process. Yet, you cannot do it alone. As an interventionist you must work with these people to gather data, do damage control, plan, and so forth. You would like for your initial ideas, conclusions, suggestions to be kept in confidence until you are certain that you have a good plan, and are ready to go public. However, given the climate of the congregation, what are your chances to find anyone who will keep your conversations confidential? The chances are zero.

There is another difficulty confronting the interventionist: the original story changes many times as it travels down the gossip trail. So, not only are your confidences broken, but what the people hear and believe does not at all resemble what you said.

Here are some principles for operating in this milieu:

A. Never try to negotiate secret plans with anyone. It never works. Such efforts will backfire and you will wind up as the identified patient.

B. Discipline yourself to keep within you those things you are aching to tell others, until you are at the place that you don't care whether they announce it throughout the congregation.

C. When you do make statements to a group, prepare a written brief of your comments and give every one a copy, so they have your comments in writing. This will lessen the chances of having your statements misconstrued.

7. DO NOT EXPECT DYSFUNCTIONAL PERSONS TO BE ABLE TO KEEP THE COMMITMENTS THEY MAKE

Addicts and codependents, identified patients and persons stuck in series relationships all have moments when they wish to do better, to get help, to get well. But until they make some progress they lack resources to do so. This always presents a particularly difficult dilemma. They must take the steps on their own or else they will make you the codependent. But what do you do if they truly do not possess the wellness needed to do it alone?

You must recruit the close members of the person's family to help the person carry out the plan — without allowing him or her to make the family into codependents. Lacking family, you may utilize close friends or, finally, yourself. But keep guard that you do not fall into a codependent role.[13]

8. RAISE AWARENESS OF FAMILY SYSTEMS THEORY AND DYSFUNCTIONAL ORGANIZATIONS

Create an awareness of what dysfunction is, what it looks like, and what its results are in the life of a congregation. Train the board, the other leaders, and as many of the congregation as you can. Have special sessions for board members and other leaders. Conduct a four or six week series for the congregation. Have a speaker from Alcoholics Anonymous or Alanon speak on the 12 Steps to Recovery. Preach on the topic; have formerly dysfunctional persons give their life story.

9. GET PROFESSIONAL COUNSEL

Working with conflicted or severely dysfunctional situations requires skill and confidence. Beyond your personal study and preparation, seek professional tutoring and counseling when you realize you are unable to handle the situation alone.[14]

10. TEND YOUR INNER LIFE

Serving a dysfunctional congregation will test your psychological, mental and spiritual mettle. Your first line of defense is to tend to your own self. Remain rested and healthy. Establish a firm routine for daily prayer and reflection. Take a day or two away each month as a time of spiritual retreat. It is said that if you draw near to the Lord, the Lord will draw near to you. We always need this nearness. When serving dysfunctional congregations, however, we need it more than ever. You must do whatever is necessary to care for yourself and your family. You would do well to reorder your priorities as follows: 1) care of myself first; 2) care of my family second, and 3) care of the congregation third.

THE TWELVE STEP RECOVERY PROGRAM OF ALCOHOLICS ANONYMOUS

The most effective process for intervening into dysfunctional congregations, or groups within the congregation, is the twelve step recovery plan, developed and used first by Alcoholics Anonymous (AA).[15] Cofounded in 1935 by William Griffith Wilson and Robert Holbrook Smith, AA's program was influenced by England's Oxford Group renewal movement in the 1920s and 1930s. The Oxford Group, declaring itself an organism, not an organization, met in hotels and homes sharing participants' spiritual life over meals. The movement based its teachings on six assumptions: 1) human beings are sinners; 2) persons can change; 3) confession is a prerequisite to change; 4) the changed soul has direct access to God; 5) the age of miracles has returned; and 6) those who have been changed are to help change others.[16]

AA cofounder William Wilson incorporated the Oxford Group's five procedures into AA's philosophy. They include: 1) giving to God; 2) listening to God's direction; 3) checking for guidance; 4) restitution; and 5) sharing, both confession and witness.[17] When Wilson and Smith attended Oxford Group meetings in New York, 1935-37, they met the leader of these meetings, Episcopal clergyperson Samuel Moor Shoemaker, Jr. The leaders in the Oxford Group, especially Shoemaker, articulated the heart of AA and its basic assumptions: self-examination, acknowledgment of character defects, and restitution for harm done.

Today this journey is utilized by many addicted and co-dependent persons, such as workaholics, overeaters, adult children of alcoholics, over spenders and sex addicts. Peace is a thematic goal for persons in recovery — the goal of the first three steps is *peace with God*; the goal of steps 4-7 is *peace with ourselves*; the goal of steps 8-10 is *peace with others*; and the goal of steps 11-12 is *keeping the peace*.[18]

Thousands of congregations in America open their doors every week to a great host of various AA based recovery programs, and this is good. However, very few members of the congregations attend any of these programs, and this is tragic. For through the doors of their church come the resources to help them deal with the dysfunctions that are resident in the congregation and its members.

THE TWELVE STEPS AND THE OTHER INTERVENTIONS

We have already discussed ten intervention ideas and principles. We will now discuss the 12 step recovery plan. The goal is not to convince you to implement the 12 steps in your congregation, but to encourage you to weave the interventions and the 12 steps like a tapestry in which the 12 steps are expressed through all of your interventions.

THE TWELVE STEPS

STEP 1: WE ADMITTED WE WERE POWERLESS OVER [AN ADDICTION] — THAT OUR LIVES HAD BECOME UNMANAGEABLE

But he said to me, "My grace is sufficient for you, for power is made perfect in weakness." So, I will boast all the more gladly of my weaknesses, so that the power of Christ may dwell in me.
(2 Cor 12:9)

Step one is about giving up control (even though people in this condition are really out of control) and dealing with the fears that go along with admitting we are powerless to rule our own lives.

Giving up an addictive behavior is not easy. It is especially hard for Christians who are cut off from their feelings, but are filled with *anxiety*. The primary response Christians first make to these feelings is *denial*. Either they will deny the reality of their feelings, since Christians aren't supposed to have such fears, angers, loneliness, temptations. Or they will deny the reality of their experience with Christ. "How can Christ be with me and I still feel these frightening urges?"

It often takes a crisis in people's lives to wake them to the reality that they are powerless over their destructive behaviors and their lives have become unmanageable.

> *Today, I ask for help with my addiction. Denial has kept me from seeing how powerless I am and how my life is unmanageable. Help me, God, to realize and remember that I have an incurable illness and that abstinence is the only way to deal with it.*[19]

*Even such as ask amiss may some-
times have their prayers answered.
The Father will never give the child a
stone that asks for bread; but I am not
sure that He will never give the child a
stone that asks for a stone. If the
Father says, "My child, that is a stone;
it is not bread," and the child answers,
"I am sure that it is bread; I want it,"
may it not be well that he should try his
"bread"?[20]* • *George MacDonald*

STEP 2: WE CAME TO BELIEVE THAT A POWER
GREATER THAN OURSELVES COULD RESTORE US
TO SANITY

*The Lord is near to the brokenhearted,
    and saves the crushed in spirit.
Many are the afflictions of the righteous,
    but the Lord rescues them from them all.*
                        (Ps 34:18-19)

*"... All things can be done for one who
    believes."* *(Mk 9:23)*

Most people who are involved in dysfunctional
conflict in the church believe that *God views the situation exactly as they do*; but what they publicly pro-
claim is that *they view the situation as God does*.
Therefore, anyone who disagrees with them is
opposing God's will for the congregation.

These people need help from God and others
to recognize the insanity of their "God and I are right;
the rest of you are wrong," position. At this step of
recovery, the congregation must be helped to realize
that its endless conflict and its accompanying pain is
not only unnecessary, it is insane, and there is little
we can do about this condition; only God's light and
truth can set us free (see John 8:32; and 9:35-41).

*Somehow I know that you can hear
me God — don't ask me how. I also
know that you can help me find my
way back...*

*I pray for an open mind so I may
come to believe in a power greater
than myself. I pray for humility and
the continued opportunity to
increase my faith. I don't want to be
crazy anymore.[21]*

STEP 3: WE MADE A DECISION TO TURN OUR
WILL AND LIVES OVER TO THE CARE OF GOD AS
WE UNDERSTOOD HIM

*Come to me, all you that are weary and are
carrying heavy burdens, and I will give you
rest. Take my yoke upon you, and learn from
me; for I am gentle and humble in heart, and
you will find rest for your souls. (Mt. 11:28-29)*

For people who are locked into dysfunctional
behaviors, the prospect of giving up control is too
large, too frightening to accomplish without the help
of God, whose power is higher than their own. The
good news is, God stands always ready to assist
those who are ready to surrender their lives up over
to the care of God.

Giving our lives to God is both a fixed reality
and a continuous process; a journey that requires
growing flexibility, trust and open communication.
The most difficult step for people in conflict is
surrendering up their judgements about the issues at
hand, so that God may lead them into unity and
truth.

*God,
I offer myself to thee, to build with
me and to do with me as you will.
Take away my difficulties, that
victory over them may bear witness
of thy power, thy love, and thy way
of life. May I do thy will always![22]*

STEP 4: WE MADE A SEARCHING AND FEARLESS MORAL INVENTORY OF OURSELVES

Search me, O God, and know my heart;
*   test me and know my thoughts.*
See if there is any wicked way in me,
*   and lead me in the way everlasting .*
*   (Ps 139:23-24)*

This step requires opening our inner selves to the grace of God so that the light of truth might shine upon the records of our lives: What have we done to exploit others? How have we deceived others? What are the fears that drive us? What is behind our constant anger? What are the results of our controlling others? Where do these come from? What do I need to learn and "face up to" from my family of origin? Who has judged, abused or manipulated me in the past and present, and how has this effected my relationships with others, even now?

> *O God of my understanding,*
> *Light a candle within my heart,*
> *That I may see what is therein*
> *And remove the wreckage of*
> *the past.[23]*

STEP 5: WE ADMITTED TO GOD, TO OURSELVES, AND TO ANOTHER HUMAN BEING THE EXACT NATURE OF OUR WRONGS

But when he came to himself he said, "How many of my father's hired hands have bread enough and to spare, but here I am dying of hunger! I will get up and go to my father, and I will say to him, "Father, I have sinned against heaven and before you; I am no longer worthy to be called your son."
*   (Lu. 17: 17-19)*

This step moves far beyond general prayers; "God forgive us we have done wrong," to a specific, lucid accounting of our actions before God. This accounting is done before God, to ourselves, and to at least one other human being. Such self disclosure of sins is urged upon us in the scriptures:

Therefore confess your sins to one another, and pray for one another, so that you may be healed. The prayer of the righteous is powerful and effective." (Ja. 5:26)

If we claim we are without sin, we deceive ourselves and the truth is not in us. (1 Jn 1:8)

> *God,*
> *I've never had to tell somebody*
> *   else about my wrongs.*
> *I've never confessed to a priest or*
> *   even to my dog.*
> *I've kept it all inside and sought to*
> *   hide.*
> *I've been too frightened to admit*
> *   what I really am.*
> *Give me courage to tell somebody*
> *   else what I've found.[24]*

STEP 6: WE WERE ENTIRELY READY TO HAVE GOD REMOVE ALL THESE DEFECTS OF CHARACTER

Come now, let us argue it out, says the Lord: though your sins are like scarlet,
*   they shall be like snow;*
though they are red like crimson,
*   they shall become like wool. (Is 1:18)*

The previous five steps of the recovery are aimed toward making people aware of their sickness and the results. These steps are intended to penetrate the people's myriad defenses and excuses — to make them aware of the need to change and what the ultimate consequences will be upon them if they do not change.

Step 6 turns the corner. It demonstrates that change of heart has occurred; people are ready for God to do spiritual surgery within and among them. This marks a turning point in the conflict, a new beginning in the people's lives. Steps 6 through 12 are intended to accomplish two things: First, to strengthen their resolve to *get* well, and to *stay* well. Second, to help those who may falter, and to spread the good news to those who have not yet heard that healing is possible.

From this step on, the pastor-as-priest will find, if he or she thinks about it, many ways to use the sacraments, the liturgical seasons, the traditions of the church to help people come into the presence of God, ask for God's help and be open to receiving the object of their requests.

> *Dear God,*
> *I don't like what I was.*
>   *But I'm not sure what I am.*
> *I was a liar.*
>   *Now I'm numb.*
> *I was a manipulator.*
>   *Now I'm empty.*
> *I was a controller.*
>   *Now I'm powerless.*
> *I was a bully.*
>   *Now I'm my own victim.*
> *I was afraid of pain.*
>   *Now I hold pain's hand.*
> *I used to hide in isolation.*
>   *Now I'm locked up with you.*
>
> *I used to be bold and loud.*
>   *Now I'm afraid to speak.*
> *I used to think only of myself.*
>   *Now I think only about the pain I've caused.*
> *I used to trust only in myself.*
>   *Now I am in your hands.*
> *O God, I'm ready, please change me.* [25]

If we confess our sins, he who is faithful and just will forgive us our sins and cleanse us from all unrighteousness.
(1 Jn 1:9)

This step emphasizes that people must move beyond contrition to confession and *metanoia* — the act of laying down their former behavior and turning their steps in a new direction. This is a change we cannot make on our own, but the grace of God is ever present to help the one who seriously wishes to change, and who asks for God's help.

Here the Lord's Supper, or a month of assigned spiritual readings, prayers, journaling — culminating in a service of joint confession and celebration will be tremendously healing.[26]

God,
Many times I have tried to change myself.
I have read books, listened to tapes, heard
*   speakers, gone on retreats, taken classes; yet*
*   I've always failed.*
I have determined to do better, scolded and
*   shamed myself, made New Year's resolutions,*
*   exercised self-control; yet I've always failed.*
I have tried everything to change; and so now I
*   come to you.*
I'm sorry that you are my last resort instead of
*   my first hope.*
I cannot boast of accomplishment, I cannot show
*   my growth, I bring you only shortcomings and*
*   needs. Please, do what I cannot do —*
*   remove these.*[27]

STEP 8: WE MADE A LIST OF EVERYONE WE HAD HARMED

Search me, o God, and know my heart,
test me and know my anxious thoughts.
(Ps. 139:23)

Zacchaeus stood there and said to the
Lord, "Look, half of my possessions, Lord, I
will give to the poor; and if I have
defrauded anyone of anything, I will pay
back four times as much. (Lk 19:8)

Step 8 is a time for searching introspection. It is a time of prayerful listening for names of persons that have been harmed by our behavior, writing down their names, and, specifically, what we did to hurt them.

> *... may I understand:*
> *To be alert to my own needs, not to*
> *   the faults of others;*
> *To remain teachable;*
> *To listen;*
> *To keep an open mind; and*
> *To learn not who's right but what's*
> *   right.[28]*

STEP 9: WE MADE DIRECT AMENDS TO SUCH PEOPLE WHEREVER POSSIBLE, EXCEPT WHEN TO DO SO WOULD INJURE THEM OR OTHERS

Let us therefore no longer pass judgment
on one another, but resolve instead never
to put a stumbling block or hindrance in the
way of another. (Rm. 14:13)

Do to others as you would have them do to
you. (Lk 6:31)

This step is the most difficult of all. However, It is absolutely essential to the healing of conflicted people, and dysfunctional relationships. This step involves getting up and going out to make heart-felt amends. Taking concrete steps is difficult — especially when our habit has been to blame others for

our faults, and to seek retribution for the wrongs done to us. Thus we kept attention focused away from our own wrongs.[29]

In working through severe conflicts, all of the previous steps will amount to nothing unless this step is carried out by the conflict parties. This requires honest, genuine contrition of heart; and going at great lengths to set things right.

This is essential not only for healing relationships, but also for addressing the substantive issues of conflict. Unresolved relational baggage builds up an emotional blockage that resists any attempt to deal with the substantive issues.

> *God,*
> *I'm scared to face some of these*
> *people to whom I am to make*
> *amends. In fact, God, I spent a*
> *great deal of effort avoiding most of*
> *the people on my list. Give me*
> *courage to face them, and this step.*
> *Let this step help me put the past*
> *behind me.[30]*

STEP 10: WE CONTINUED TO TAKE PERSONAL INVENTORY AND WHEN WE WERE WRONG PROMPTLY ADMITTED IT

You were taught to put away your former
way of life, your old self...and to clothe
yourselves with your new self.
(Eph 4:22a, 24a)

This step emphasizes that healing from addiction and codependency is a continuing journey, not a one time event. Jesus invited his followers to take up their cross *daily* and follow him (Lk 9:23). Daily inventory, reflection and *examination of consciousness*[31] are necessary for our continued healing and growth.

If our recovery is from *resentment*, for example, we will know we are making progress when we feel greater tolerance for others, take responsibility for our own feelings, and let go of the need to retaliate. If we are in recovery from *fear*, we will know it is happening when we feel more joy, embrace change, and feel less threatened. We know that we are in a process of recovering from *inappropriate anger* when we can make reasonable requests, appropriately express anger, or set limits for ourselves. Recovering from *approval seeking* begins when we recognize our own needs, tell the truth about how we feel, stop rescuing or taking care of others. Recovery from *control* begins when we take steps to trust others, empower others, accept others as they are without wanting to change them.[32]

I pray that I may continue:
To grow in understanding and
effectiveness;
To take daily spot check inventories
of myself;
To correct mistakes when I make
them;
To take responsibility for my actions;
To be ever aware of my negative
and self-defeating attitudes and
behaviors;
To keep my willfulness in check;
To always remember I need your
help;
To keep love and tolerance of others
as my code; and
To continue in daily prayer to know
how I can best serve you.[33]

STEP 11: *WE SOUGHT THROUGH PRAYER AND MEDITATION TO IMPROVE OUR CONSCIOUS CONTACT WITH GOD, PRAYING ONLY FOR POWER TO CARRY THAT OUT*[34]

And when you turn to the right or when you turn to the left, your ears shall hear a word behind you, saying, "This is the way; walk in it." (Is 30:21)

By now the person in recovery has faced up to his or her sickness, and has taken the steps to be healed. What remains is to develop a daily discipline to reinforce their healing — every day. This step is intended to keep people from returning to former patterns of dysfunctional relationships by replacing their old habits with new habits. This can only be done by building into one's life daily habits that bring to each day a new consciousness of Christ's presence; so we know that,

all our desires, thoughts, and actions are constantly guided by him. When we walk in the Lord's presence, everything we see, hear, touch, or taste reminds us of him. ... It is not a life in which we say many prayers, but a life in which nothing, absolutely nothing, is done, said, or understood independently of [God] who is the origin and purpose of our existence.[35]

Dear God,
You know my needs before I ask,
my heart before I pray, and
my gratitude before I even offer
my thanks.
You understand me better than I
understand myself,
and I thank you for
communicating with me in the
language of the heart.[36]

STEP 12: HAVING HAD A SPIRITUAL AWAKENING AS THE RESULT OF THESE STEPS, WE TRIED TO CARRY THIS MESSAGE TO OTHERS, AND TO PRACTICE THESE PRINCIPLES IN ALL OUR AFFAIRS

No one after lighting a lamp hides it under a jar, or puts it under a bed, but puts it on a lampstand so that those who enter may see the light. (Lk 8:16)

The last step is based upon the conviction that the best defense against relapsing into former behavior is to continually share the good news of one's recovery with others who are still caught in dysfunctional behavior, and working with them to affect their healing.

This is evangelism in its purest form: a person who struggles with a specific malady carrying the good news to someone who struggles with the same affliction. In Christ, those who are healed become healers — and they remain healed in the process.

> *God, grant me the serenity*
> *to accept the things I cannot change,*
> *the courage to change the things I can,*
> *and the wisdom to know the difference.*
> *Living one day at a time,*
> *enjoying one moment at a time;*
> *accepting hardship as a pathway to peace;*
> *taking, as Jesus did,*
> *this sinful world as it is,*
> *not as I would have it;*
> *trusting that You will make all things right*
> *if I surrender to your will;*
> *so that I may be reasonably happy in this life*
> *and supremely happy with You*
> *forever in the next. Amen*
> *• Reinhold Neibuhr*

The twelve steps are most appropriate for use with a congregation or church group which has become addictive in its behaviors and relationships. The orientation of the twelve steps is 'God-ward,' and the processes are familiar to every Christian; repentance, confession, prayer, restitution, metanoia, commitment, trust in God to provide the strength needed day-by-day and evangelism.

One advantage of using the twelve steps with congregations is that there are many persons in every community who are familiar, skilled and experienced in the processes for utilizing the twelve steps with groups. These persons can become your consultants and trainers in working with dysfunctional families or groups. These are the leaders of a growing variety of twelve step groups who have a good reputation for their effectiveness.

The 'tools' and guidelines discussed in this chapter will help you plan your comprehensive intervention strategies. The first set of tools presented in this chapter come from the understandings of Family Systems Theory. The 12 steps is the intervention model of all 12 step recovery groups working with persons who suffer various addictions.

Your interventions will be most effective when you:

1. First think through the situation in light of the materials presented in this book and then,
2. Plan your interventions utilizing combinations of the intervention materials presented in this chapter.

Pray that you may never have to intervene into the lives of dysfunctional persons or congregations. However, as American society continues to exhibit signs of dysfunction among its citizens, the chances are you will sooner or later work in a congregation that needs the things you have learned in this study.

---

[1] Michael H. Crosby, *The Dysfunctional Church: Addiction and Co-dependency in the Family of Catholicism* (Notre Dame, IN: Ave Maria Press, 1991), p. 7.

[2] R. Paul Stevens and Phil Collins, *The Equipping Pastor: A Systems Approach to Congregational Leadership* (Washington, DC: The Alban Institute, 1993), p. xv.

[3] Following these definitions, the Sunday sermon is probably the most common intervention into the life of the church, although we all have heard some that seemed to be more like accidents. We can learn how to plan and carry out interventions. Most of us already know how to do accidents.

[4] Chris Argyris is a professor at Harvard University. He is one of the best consultants in the world.

[5] The church is perhaps the organization that most violates these principles. Every day in America churches make thousands of decisions for which the people have not been provided valid and understandable information. Under such circumstances, matters can only get worse.

[6] See Chris Argyris: *Intervention Theory & Method* (Reading: Addison-Wesley Publishing, 1970). See also, Chris Argyris & Donald Schön, *Organizational Learning: A Theory of Action Perspective*, (1978).

[7] Robert Blake & Jane Mouton: *Consultation* (Reading: Addison -Wesley Publishing, 1976).

[8] Taken from, Anne Wilson Shaef, "Is the Church an Addictive System? "*The Christian Century*, 3-10 January, 1990, pp. 18-21; also see Anne Wilson Schaef and Dianne Fassel. *The Addictive Organization* (San Francisco: Harper & Row, 1988).

GREAT

resources

GREAT

resources

[9] Anne Wilson Shaef, "Is the Church an Addictive System?" *The Christian Century*, 3-10 January, 1990, pp. 18-19.

[10] Edwin H. Friedman, *Generation to Generation: Family Process In Church And Synagogue* (New York: The Guilford Press, 1985), p. 208.

[11] Edwin H. Friedman, *Generation to Generation: Family Process In Church And Synagogue*, p. 209.

[12] Kenneth Hauck, *Antagonists in the Church: How to Identify and Deal with Destructive Conflict* (Minneapolis: Augsburg Publishing House, 1988.)

[13] I learned this principle the hard way. I consulted a pastor who was severely dysfunctional; the congregation was riddled with dysfunction and conflict. After much work I convinced the pastor to enter a institution for pastors suffering psychological illness. After days of terrible fighting I convinced the congregation not to fire him, but to fund his treatment at the institution. The pastor took the money and left for the hospital. He never got there. In six weeks he returned to the church, as sick as ever, and announced to the congregation that he had spent the six weeks in Hawaii. The congregation fired him. I learned a lesson that I will never forget.

[14] There are agencies and consulting firms that are available to assist you in working with dysfunctional congregations; for example, the authors are associated with Shawchuck & Associates, Ltd., a consulting company that works intensively in church conflict management.

[15] There are many materials available for persons interested in recovery programs. For example, see *The Twelve Steps A Spiritual Journey: A Working Guide for Healing Damaged Emotions* (San Diego: RPI Publishing, 1988, 1994); *Prayers for The Twelve Steps -- A Spiritual Journey* (San Diego: Recovery Publications, 1993); *The Twelve Steps for Christians* (San Diego: RPI Publishing, 1988, 1994); Martin M. Davis, *The Gospel and the Twelve Steps: Developing A Closer Relationship With Jesus* (San Diego: RPI Publishing, 1993); Jerry Seiden, *Divine Or Distorted: God As We Understand God* (San Diego: Recovery Publications, 1993); and Don Williams, *Jesus and Addiction: A Prescription to Transform the Dysfunctional Church and Recover Authentic Christianity* (San Diego: Recovery Publications, 1993):

[16] Hadley Cantril, *The Psychology of Social Movements* (Huntington, NY: Robert E. Kruger, 1941), pp. 147-148, in *The Twelve Steps A Spiritual Journey: A Working Guide for Healing Damaged Emotions* (San Diego: RPI Publishing, 1988, 1994), pp. ix, x.

[17] Ernest Kurtz, *Not God: A History of Alcoholics Anonymous* (Century City, MN: Hazelden Educational Materials, 1979), pp. 48-49, in *The Twelve Steps A Spiritual Journey: A Working Guide for Healing Damaged Emotions* (San Diego: RPI Publishing, 1988, 1994), p. x..

[18] *The Twelve Steps A Spiritual Journey: A Working Guide for Healing Damaged Emotions* (San Diego: RPI Publishing, 1988, 1994), p. xii.

[19] *Prayers for The Twelve Steps -- A Spiritual Journey* (San Diego: Recovery Publications, 1993), p. 8.

[20] George MacDonald, *365 Readings*, edited by C.S. Lewis (New York: Collier Books, MacMillan Publishing, 1947), pp. 46-47.

[21] *Prayers for The Twelve Steps -- A Spiritual Journey* (San Diego: Recovery Publications, 1993), p. 10.

[22] *Prayers for The Twelve Steps -- A Spiritual Journey* (San Diego: Recovery Publications, 1993), p. 12.

[23] *Prayers for The Twelve Steps -- A Spiritual Journey* (San Diego: Recovery Publications, 1993), p. 14.

[24] *Prayers for The Twelve Steps -- A Spiritual Journey* (San Diego: Recovery Publications, 1993), pp. 16-17.

[25] *Prayers for The Twelve Steps -- A Spiritual Journey* (San Diego: Recovery Publications, 1993), pp. 18-19.

[26] For use of the Lord's Supper with conflicted groups, I have found no liturgy better than A Service of Word and Table #IV, see The United Methodist Hymnal (Nashville: The United Methodist Publishing House, 1989), pp. 26-31.

[27] *Prayers for The Twelve Steps -- A Spiritual Journey* (San Diego: Recovery Publications, 1993), pp. 20-21.

[28] *Prayers for The Twelve Steps -- A Spiritual Journey* (San Diego: Recovery Publications, 1993), pp. 22-23.

[29] *The Twelve Steps for Christians* (San Diego: RPI Publishing, 1988, 1994), p. 130.

[30] *Prayers for The Twelve Steps -- A Spiritual Journey* (San Diego: Recovery Publications, 1993), pp. 20-24.

[31] The examen of consciousness is a time of prayer, perhaps fifteen minutes once or twice daily, and is concerned with what happens in our consciousness prior to our actions, events or conditions. See George A. Aschenbrenner, "Consciousness Examen," in *Review for Religious* 31.1 (1972): 15; also see our book, *Leading the Congregation: Caring for Yourself While Serving Others* (Nashville: Abingdon Press, 1993), pp. 51-55.

[32] *The Twelve Steps for Christians* (San Diego: RPI Publishing, 1988, 1994), pp. 169-183.

[33] *Prayers for The Twelve Steps -- A Spiritual Journey* (San Diego: Recovery Publications, 1993), pp. 20-26.

[34] Perhaps the best resource for helping people do this are *A Guide to Prayer for Ministers and Other Servants*, or *A Guide to Prayer for All God's People*. These books present lead persons into prayer and meditation through the use of weekly and daily resources. See, Rueben Job and Norman Shawchuck, (Nashville: The Upper Room).

[35] Henri J.M. Nouwen, *The Living Reminder: Service and Prayer In Memory of Jesus Christ* (Minneapolis: The Seabury Press, 1977), pp. 31, 28.

[36] *Prayers for The Twelve Steps -- A Spiritual Journey* (San Diego: Recovery Publications, 1993), p. 29.

POSTLUDE

The dysfunctional conditions and their results included in this little book do not come from my head — they come from my gut. I have experienced all of these dynamics in my work as a management consultant to religious organizations.

I believe that God's people in the world, however unhealthy or healthy, are all doing the best they can. They all love God, as I do, and yearn to see God, as I do. Yet many of them exact great pain upon themselves and others. The social cost of dysfunction in the church is incalculable. Pastors and families are forced to uproot themselves altogether too often, long time members grieve to see their beloved church in chaos and pain.

Congregations are tough. Even the dysfunctional ones manage to survive. But every congregation deserves better than to merely survive in a mileau of pain, anger and brokenness.

God knows this, and continues to call pastors and lay people to serve and suffer with congregations that are in dysfunction. When you find yourself in a dysfunctional church, don't leave it. Love it. But above all, heal it.

You can do it. It may cost you and your family a lot, but no more than the cost Jesus bore in order to heal us all. And Jesus will never leave you there alone. Even in the most dysfunctional church with which I have worked, I have sensed Jesus there — loving them, holding them in a prevailing grace.

Jesus has stuck by me and loved me when I tried to bring healing and failed. And Jesus has urged me not to give up. Jesus has urged me to pay the price of learning, thinking, doing — over and over again until I discover how to do it right. I now understand that what Jesus is doing in me, and through me, makes every cost a currency well spent.

For years I have taught and counselled pastors and lay persons, "When you find yourself in a conflicted, failing church remember you can leave tomorrow — only don't leave until you have brought it to a better condition than when you arrived." I think this counsel is from the heart of Jesus, who came into our world — and didn't leave it until he had set in motion the principles and practices for healing. This he did at great cost. Yet he never abandoned the dysfunctional, the blind, lame and down right mean.

Let's live out our calling in the light of his example.

We heal others out of our own brokenness. God uses the point of our greatest pain as the source of our greatest healing of others. I have lived long enough to see this in my own life. I guess this means that Jesus, the Great Redeemer, can redeem even the dysfunction of our lives.

ABOUT THE AUTHOR...

If you have heard of the proverb, "People tend to support what they help to create," you already know a little about the author, Dr. Norman Shawchuck.

He is the president of Shawchuck and Associates, Ltd., specializing in management consulting to religious organizations nationally and internationally; conducting research into religious organizations; and offering training seminars in leadership, conflict management, marketing and spiritual formation.

Dr. Shawchuck is the author/co-author of several books on church leadership and spiritual formation including Managing the Congregation: Building Effective Systems to Serve People, Benchmarks of Quality in the Church: 21 Ways to Continuously Improve the Content of Your Ministry, Leading the Congregations: Caring for Yourself While Serving the People, A Guide to Prayer For All God's People, A Guide to Prayer For Ministers and Other Servants, Marketing for the Church: Choosing to Serve People More Effectively, How to Conduct a Spiritual Life Retreat, How To Be A More Effective Church Leader, What it Means To Be A Church Leader, How To Manage Conflict In The Church, Management For Your Church, Let My People Go: Empowering Laity For Ministry and Revitalizing the 20th Century Church. He is a contributing editor for Leadership: A Practical Journal For Church Leaders. He has authored scores of articles and research papers.

He serves on the doctoral faculties of numerous theological seminaries, and teaches in the fields of religious leadership and spirituality. He is a Research Scholar on the faculty of the school of Industrial Engineering, Northwestern University.